ACCESS AWARD IN BOOKKEEPING

STUDY TEXT 2020/21

Qualifications and Credit Framework

AAT Level 1

British Library Cataloguing-in-Publication Data

A catalogue record for this book is available from the British Library.

Published by
Kaplan Publishing UK
Unit 2, The Business Centre
Molly Millars Lane
Wokingham
Berkshire
RG41 2QZ

ISBN 978 1 78740 832 6

Printed and bound in Great Britain.

Kaplan Publishing would like to thank Angela Renshaw and Deborah Seed for their contributions towards the production of this publication.

KAPLAN PUBLISHING

CONTENTS

INTRODUCTION

HOW TO USE THESE MATERIALS

These Kaplan Publishing learning materials have been carefully designed to make your learning experience as easy as possible and to give you the best chance of success in your AAT assessments.

They contain a number of features to help you in the study process.

The sections on the Unit Guide, the Assessment and Study Skills should be read before you commence your studies.

They are designed to familiarise you with the nature and content of the assessment and to give you tips on how best to approach your studies.

STUDY TEXT

This Study Text has been specially prepared for the revised AAT Access qualification introduced in 2018.

It is written in a practical and interactive style by expert classroom tutors.

In this Study Text:

- key terms and concepts are clearly defined

- all topics are illustrated with practical examples with clearly worked solutions based on sample tasks provided by the AAT in the new assessment style

- frequent activities throughout and at the end of the chapters ensure that what you have learnt is regularly reinforced

- 'Test your understanding' activities are included within each chapter to apply your learning and develop your understanding

- a 'Case Study' brings the subject to life and puts the content covered into a real life context

- Mock Assessments and end of chapter activities reinforce understanding to prepare you for the assessment.

ICONS

The chapters include the following icons throughout.

They are designed to assist you in your studies by identifying key definitions and the points at which you can test yourself on the knowledge gained.

Definition

These sections explain important areas of Knowledge which must be understood and reproduced in an assessment

Example

The illustrative examples can be used to help develop an understanding of topics before attempting the activity exercises

Test your understanding

These are exercises which give the opportunity to assess your understanding of all the assessment areas.

Case study

These examples put the chapter content into a real life context, using the case study of Jessica and her role at How Two Ltd.

Case study activities

Following the chapter summary, these questions enable further practice using the real life context of the above case study.

UNIT GUIDE

Introduction

The AAT Access Award in Bookkeeping offers students at Level 1 the opportunity to develop practical bookkeeping skills. This qualification may help students to move on to further study in either accountancy or bookkeeping with AAT, offer a route into employment or be of interest to those already in employment.

This qualification will particularly suit those students who have had minimal work experience or those who need some additional support in order to progress. This qualification may also interest those who are self-employed or working in small businesses who wish to do their own bookkeeping.

Students should choose to study the AAT Access Award in Bookkeeping if they wish to develop an understanding of the basics of manual bookkeeping. This qualification complements the other qualifications in the suite of AAT Access qualifications and may be combined with the AAT Access Award in Accounting Software to lay a strong foundation for further study with AAT in either accountancy or bookkeeping.

A student completing this qualification will develop an understanding of the role of the bookkeeper, including the need for confidentiality and accuracy in their work. The qualification also covers underpinning theory including how to identify assets, liabilities, income and expenses; how to identify profit and loss; and the differences between trading for cash and trading on credit.

Students will also develop the skills to process customer and supplier transactions, to enter receipts and payments into the cash book and check amounts against the bank statement in preparation for bank reconciliation and will also be introduced to the dual effect of transactions. This is a fundamental underpinning concept for double-entry bookkeeping and will support students who go on to study bookkeeping at Foundation level.

The skills developed in this qualification can lead to employment in junior or supporting administrative roles in companies across a wide range of sectors, for example, as a:

- trainee bookkeeper
- accounts administrator
- billing/payments administrator/coordinator
- accounts junior
- accounts receivable/payable assistant
- procurement and finance assistant
- assistant cashier.

Overview and learning outcomes

Overview

The AAT Access Award in Bookkeeping introduces students to the role of the bookkeeper and simple bookkeeping techniques. It covers the buying and selling process and the common documents used. It also includes recording transactions in the books of prime entry.

On completion of this unit, students will be familiar with bookkeeping terminology and will have developed practical bookkeeping skills. Students will gain the confidence to contribute effectively in the workplace and to move on to further study in bookkeeping.

They will learn the difference between assets, liabilities, income and expenses. They will discover that every transaction has a dual effect within the bookkeeping system. While this unit does not include the double-entry bookkeeping system, it will prepare students to learn double-entry bookkeeping skills, either in future studies or at work.

Students will also be able to prepare customer invoices and credit notes, to check supplier invoices and credit notes and to record these documents in the relevant books of prime entry. They will be able to calculate amounts owing from customers and to suppliers.

Students will be able to use an analysed cash book to record receipts and payments. They will calculate amounts of cash in hand and cash in the bank. They will be able to check the cash book against the bank statement and identify any differences.

Learning outcomes

The Access Award in Bookkeeping comprises of four learning outcomes:

1. Understand the role of the bookkeeper
2. Understand financial transactions
3. Process customer and supplier transactions
4. Process receipts and payments

Scope of content and assessment criteria

Understand the role of the bookkeeper (Chapters 1, 4 & 5)

1.1 Duties and responsibilities of a bookkeeper

Students need to know:

- that bookkeepers prepare and check financial documentation
- that bookkeepers record and check financial transactions
- that bookkeepers are required to keep information confidential
- that bookkeepers must refer to a supervisor or seek authorisation when appropriate.

1.2 Ways to keep information confidential

Students need to know:

- that passwords can be used to keep information confidential
- types of secure storage for soft-copy and hard-copy information
- the importance of sharing information with authorised personnel only.

1.3 Importance of working with accuracy

Students need to know the potential effect of bookkeeping errors:

- incorrect accounting records – overstatement, understatement
- incorrect profit/loss
- delayed receipts from customers
- duplicated payments to suppliers
- incorrect payments to suppliers – overpayment, underpayment
- delayed receipt of goods from suppliers
- incorrect information on internal/external reports
- time spent tracing and correcting errors.

Understand financial transactions (Chapters 2, 3 & 6)

2.1 The buying and selling process

Students need to know:

- the difference between trading for cash and trading on credit:
  - cash sales
  - cash purchases
  - credit sales
  - credit purchases
  - customers
  - suppliers
  - trade receivables
  - trade payables
- relevant documents and how they are used:
  - sales and purchase invoice
  - sales and purchase credit note
  - quotation
  - purchase order
  - delivery note
  - goods received note
  - goods returned note
  - cash receipt
  - remittance advice.

2.2 Basic bookkeeping terminology

Students need to know:

- the meaning of:
  - assets
  - liabilities
  - income
  - expenses
- how to identify items as:
  - assets
  - liabilities
  - income
  - expenses

KAPLAN PUBLISHING

- the meaning of profit and loss: income minus expenses
- how to identify when there is a profit and when there is a loss.

2.3   The dual effect of transactions

Students need to know:

- that items that can be classified as assets, liabilities, income or expenses are recorded in the bookkeeping system
- that each transaction changes the records of at least two items in the bookkeeping system: item amounts may increase and/or decrease.

Process customer and supplier transactions (Chapters 3 & 5)

3.1   Prepare sales invoices and credit notes

Students need to know:

- the documents used to prepare sales invoices and credit notes:
    - quotation
    - delivery note
    - price list.

Students must be able to:

- complete documents used in the sales process (delivery note, sales invoice) with:
    - customer name
    - customer address
    - invoice number
    - invoice date
    - credit note number
    - credit note date
    - product description
    - product code
- complete sales invoice and credit note amounts:
    - unit price and price for multiple units
    - discounts for buying in large quantities
    - amounts (net, VAT and total)

3.2   Check purchase invoices and credit notes

Students need to know:

- the documents used to check purchase invoices and credit notes:
  - purchase order
  - goods received note
  - goods returned note.

Students must be able to:

- identify errors:
  - VAT amounts
  - Calculations
  - type of goods
  - quantity of goods
  - unit price.

3.3   Record sales and purchase invoices and credit notes in the books of prime entry

Students need to know:

- the books of prime entry:
  - sales day book
  - purchases day book
  - sales returns day book
  - purchases returns day book.
- the columns within the books of prime entry:
  - date
  - customer/supplier name
  - customer/supplier invoice number/credit note number
  - amounts (net, VAT and total).

Students must be able to:

- make entries in the books of prime entry
- total columns in the books of prime entry
- cross cast columns in the books of prime entry.

3.4 Identify outstanding amounts for individual customers and suppliers

Students need to know:

- the documents used:
    - sales and purchase invoices
    - sales and purchase credit notes
    - lists of invoices and/or credit notes
    - cheque stubs
    - cash receipts
    - remittance advices
    - lists of receipts and/or payments.
- the records used:
    - sales day book
    - purchases day book
    - sales returns day book
    - purchases returns day book.

Students must be able to:

- calculate amounts owed by customers
- calculate amounts owed to suppliers
- use an opening amount owed.

Process receipts and payments (Chapters 5 & 7)

4.1 Enter receipts and payments into a cash book

Students need to know:

- the format of the cash book:
    - receipts side
    - payments side
- the columns within the cash book:
    - date
    - customer/supplier
    - cash and/or bank
    - analysis columns (including VAT analysis)
- the documents used:
    - cash receipts
    - cheque stubs
    - remittance advices
    - lists of receipts and/or payments
    - lists of Direct Debits and/or standing orders
    - lists of Faster Payments and/or BACS.

Students must be able to:

- make entries in the cash book:
    - receipts
    - payments
    - total columns in the cash book
    - cross cast columns in the cash book.

4.2 Use the cash book to calculate closing amounts of cash in hand and cash in the bank

Students must be able to:

- calculate the closing amount of cash in hand from the opening amount, amounts received and amounts paid
- calculate the closing amount of cash in the bank from the opening amount, amounts received and amounts paid.

4.3 Checking the closing amount of cash in the bank against the closing balance on the bank statement

Students must be able to:

- identify receipts and payments on the bank statement
  - counter credits
  - standing orders
  - Direct Debits
  - cheques
  - BACS
  - Faster Payments
  - bank charges
  - bank interest received.
- identify balances on the bank statement
- identify items in the cash book that are not on the bank statement
- identify items on the bank statement that are not in the cash book.

The assessment

Assessment for this award will be by Computer based assessment (CBA), with a mixture of computer-marked tasks, including multiple choice, true/false, drag and drop, drop-down lists, calculation and completion of relevant forms.

The assessment will be under timed conditions. The timed allowed for the assessment is 90 minutes.

The assessment is wholly computer-marked.

The weighting of the learning outcomes is as follows:

1. Understand the role of the bookkeeper	10%
2. Understand financial transactions	15%
3. Process customer and supplier transactions	35%
4. Process receipts and payments	40%
Total	100%

STUDY SKILLS

Preparing to study

Devise a study plan

Determine which times of the week you will study.

Split these times into sessions of at least one hour for study of new material. Any shorter periods could be used for revision or practice.

Put the times you plan to study onto a study plan for the weeks from now until the assessment and set yourself targets for each period of study – in your sessions make sure you cover the whole course, activities and the associated questions with answers at the back of the Study Text.

When working through your course, compare your progress with your plan and, if necessary, re-plan your work (perhaps including extra sessions) or, if you are ahead, do some extra revision/practice questions.

Effective studying

Active reading

You are not expected to learn the text by rote, rather, you must understand what you are reading and be able to use it to pass the assessment and develop good practice.

A good technique is to use SQ3Rs – Survey, Question, Read, Recall, Review:

1   **Survey the chapter**

Look at the headings and read the introduction, knowledge, skills and content, so as to get an overview of what the chapter deals with.

2   **Question**

Whilst undertaking the survey ask yourself the questions you hope the chapter will answer for you.

3   **Read**

Read through the chapter thoroughly working through the activities and, at the end, making sure that you can meet the learning objectives shown within the summary.

4   **Recall**

At the end of each chapter, try to recall the main ideas of the section/chapter without referring to the text. This is best done after short break of a couple of minutes after the reading stage.

5   **Review**

Check that your recall notes are correct.

You may also find it helpful to re-read the chapter to try and see the topic(s) it deals with as a whole.

Note taking

Taking notes is a useful way of learning, but do not simply copy out the text. The notes must:

- be in your own words
- be concise
- cover the key points
- be well organised
- be modified as you study further chapters in this text or in related ones.

Trying to summarise a chapter without referring to the text can be a useful way of determining which areas you know and which you don't.

Three ways of taking notes

1   **Summarise the key points of a chapter**

2   **Make linear notes**

A list of headings, subdivided with sub-headings listing the key points.

If you use linear notes, you can use different colours to highlight key points and keep topic areas together.

Use plenty of space to make your notes easy to use.

3   **Try a diagrammatic form**

The most common of which is a mind map.

To make a mind map, put the main heading in the centre of the paper and put a circle around it.

Draw lines radiating from this to the main sub-headings which again have circles around them.

Continue the process from the sub-headings to sub-sub-headings.

Highlighting and underlining

You may find it useful to underline or highlight key points in your study text – but do be selective.

You may also wish to make notes in the margins.

Further reading

In addition to this text, you should also read the 'Student section' of the 'Accounting Technician' magazine every month to keep abreast of any guidance from the examiners.

The role of a bookkeeper

1

Introduction

In this chapter we will look at the role of a bookkeeper and what it entails. Having established the different tasks carried out by a bookkeeper, it will become clear why they play such a vital role in an accounting function.

As information provided by accounting professionals may be commercially sensitive, it is also important to understand why a bookkeeper needs to know how to handle this data confidentially.

Finally, we will look at the importance of bookkeepers keeping their knowledge up to date and what their professional and ethical responsibilities are.

KNOWLEDGE	CONTENTS
Understand the role of a bookkeeper 1.1 Duties and responsibilities of a bookkeeper 1.2 Ways to keep information confidential	1 The duties and responsibilities of a bookkeeper 2 Confidentiality and data security 3 Summary and further questions

1   Duties and responsibilities of a bookkeeper

1.1   Case study: an introduction

📖 Case study

Jessica has completed full-time education and, having gained some work experience in her uncle's shop, she is keen to pursue a career in accountancy. She has always enjoyed mathematics and has a good eye for detail.

Jessica has started an apprenticeship with the finance department at How Two Ltd, a supplier of computer components. As a result of the knowledge and skills she has acquired during her apprenticeship, Jessica has been given the task, as a junior bookkeeper, of getting all the financial records at How Two up to date. Jessica's manager stresses the need to ensure that the records balance accurately and to complete the task in a timely manner.

Jessica considers the importance of her role as a bookkeeper and the factors she needs to think about when completing this task.

Her progress will be monitored and checked by her mentor as Jessica completes a series of activities to ensure that she fully understands.

1.2   Why do we need bookkeepers?

📖 Case study

One of the reasons that Jessica entered the accounting profession, and one of the first things she learnt when she started working in the finance department at How Two Ltd, was that *no matter where you live or work in the world, an organisation will always need a bookkeeper.*

The main reasons bookkeepers will always be needed are:

- So that the owner/manager knows the income and expenditure of the business.
- So that the owner/manager can make decisions that will improve/expand the business.
- So that the organisation pays the correct amount of taxes due.

All governments need money to finance their activities, and they obtain that money from businesses and individuals in the form of taxes.

1.3 The role of the bookkeeper

The role of the bookkeeper is to keep an accurate record of all financial transactions carried out by an organisation. In most organisations, a bookkeeper will be required to prepare and check financial documentation before recording the financial transactions.

Every financial transaction is first recorded in a daybook and then transferred to ledgers. Details of this process will be covered further on in this Study Text, but for now it is imperative that you understand it is the bookkeeper's role to record and check financial transactions. Ultimately, they are responsible for keeping the accounting records up to date and accurate.

> **Example**
>
> A bookkeeper checks the details of purchase orders against delivery notes which state what goods have been delivered to the customer. If the delivery note has been signed by the customer and everything agrees, the bookkeeper is then required to prepare a sales invoice to be sent to the customer, checking that it is accurate before sending it out.

In larger organisations, the bookkeeping work is often separated into different business activities carried out by clerks.

> **Example**
>
> A sales ledger clerk will produce customer invoices and statements and chase up outstanding debts.
>
> A purchases ledger clerk will keep a record of all invoices received from suppliers and process payments.
>
> Cashiers are responsible for recording all monies received and paid by the business.
>
> **In smaller organisations, a bookkeeper will perform all of these activities.**

Once the data has been entered, the information will be analysed by an accountant who will produce financial reports for the owner/manager of the business to enable them to make business decisions.

Accountants are also given the power to authorise certain transactions within a business whereas a bookkeeper simply processes them.

Accountants help this decision-making process by interpreting and offering alternative strategies.

The accounting function provides help and support to all other functions within the organisation. The managers of these other functions will rely on the information provided by accounting staff in order to run their departments effectively and contribute to the overall smooth running of the organisation.

Therefore, it is essential that the information provided by bookkeepers or accounts clerks is accurate (free from errors), up to date and complete (nothing is missing). If there is something that a bookkeeper is unsure of, or that they feel is outside of the scope of their role, it is vital that they refer to their supervisor/manager for advice or seek approval from the accountant before acting upon it.

1.4　Information from the accounting function

The table below gives examples of the key information provided by the accounts department to other functions in the organisation.

Information	Function
Management will need information about the profit or loss of the organisation. For example, they may want to know whether a particular product is making a profit or a loss, or which department is making the most profit.	Management
The manager of the production department may want to know if the department has spent more or less than budgeted. They may need to know the cost of raw materials, discounts, the cost of any machinery and the budget for any replacements.	Production
The sales function may want to know about the income received from a particular product or the level of sales each sales person has been responsible for.	Sales
Human Resources may want the total salary cost of the staff, if there is a recruitment budget and whether there are any bonuses, overtime or commission due.	Human Resources

1.5　Continuing Professional Development (CPD)

Bookkeepers and accounts clerks are entry level job roles, but there are a lot of opportunities for career progression by work experience and gaining bookkeeping and accounting qualifications.

A bookkeeper is responsible for their own continuing professional development. Continuing professional development is where an individual enhances or maintains their professional skills and experience to keep their knowledge of their chosen profession up to date.

When considering their professional development, bookkeepers will need to assess and look to develop their skills. Some of their career skills are professional, whereas some are their personal attributes. Professional skills include:

Professionalism Accounting professionals should be able to demonstrate a high level of competence in their work and be able to meet the required standards of the profession.

Integrity Accounting professionals should adopt an approach to work guided by strong moral principles. They are expected to be straightforward, honest and trustworthy.

Numeracy Accounting professionals are expected to have good numeracy skills. They should be able to process numerical information quickly and accurately and be able to understand and explain calculations.

Literacy Accounting professionals need to be skilled at dealing with written content.

Communication Skills Accounting professionals need to be able to speak and deal with a wide range of people using a range of communication skills: e.g. writing, speaking, presenting, and listening.

As well as the key skills mentioned above, accounting professionals are expected to display certain personal attributes. These include:

Reliability Employers and your team workers will need to rely on you to do the work that you promised to do.

Punctuality Being punctual means being on time, both in terms of arriving at your place of work on time and completing a required task at an agreed time.

Willingness to learn Showing a willingness to learn demonstrates that you are interested in your job role and the organisation. It also suggests you are not afraid of learning new skills which will help you and the organisation to develop.

Organisation Employers will expect you to be able to complete work within an agreed time frame. If you are well-organised you are more likely to be able to complete your work effectively and efficiently.

New skills and knowledge can be acquired in a variety of ways.

Accounting professionals will undertake **formal training** to learn technical skills, for example by enrolling on a college course to take AAT qualifications. Knowledge and experience can also be acquired through

informal training such as self-study or on the job training. Examples of informal training are given below.

🔅 Example

Job Rotation	Job rotation involves switching employees round through a range of jobs. Job rotation can mean that employees are given a wider knowledge of the organisation. It can also help the organisation if cover is needed for absent staff.
Job Shadowing	Job shadowing means working with an experienced employee who can pass on the skills and knowledge required to perform the task
Professional Journals	Professional journals are magazines written by professionals in a particular field of interest. For example, the AAT Accounting Technician magazine.
Internet/ newspapers	These sources provide up to date financial news and information relevant to accounting professionals.

The AAT's Continuing Professional Development (CPD) policy follows a four-stage cycle: Assess, Plan, Action, Evaluate. The AAT recommend that the cycle is followed at least twice each year in order for its members to develop their skills and further their career.

When considering their personal development, the AAT CPD cycle can help bookkeepers and their line managers to evaluate your performance and set appropriate development goals and targets. It also will enable them to continually assess their learning needs to keep up to date with professional developments.

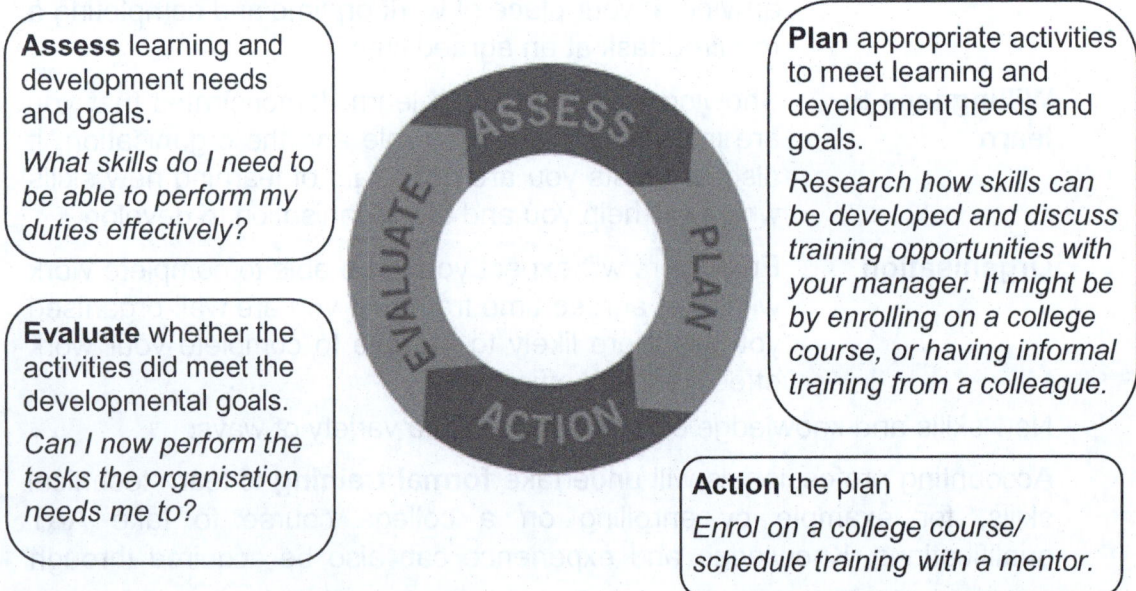

Assess learning and development needs and goals.

What skills do I need to be able to perform my duties effectively?

Plan appropriate activities to meet learning and development needs and goals.

Research how skills can be developed and discuss training opportunities with your manager. It might be by enrolling on a college course, or having informal training from a colleague.

Evaluate whether the activities did meet the developmental goals.

Can I now perform the tasks the organisation needs me to?

Action the plan

Enrol on a college course/ schedule training with a mentor.

ASSESS PLAN ACTION EVALUATE

✎ Test your understanding 1

Fill in the gaps from the pick list below to complete the paragraph about bookkeepers.

The bookkeeper is responsible for _____ the financial _____ of an organisation. An accountant is responsible for _____ the financial _____ of an organisation.

The _____ suggests alternative strategies, based on the interpretation of the financial information. The _____ will make the decisions.

A bookkeeper may start as a _____, but, with hard work and study, can progress to _____ accountant.

Pick list

Accountant	bookkeeper	information	interpreting
manager	senior	inputting	transactions

✎ Test your understanding 2

Below is a list of duties that are performed in the accounting department. Tick the column to suggest who would typically perform each task.

Role	Bookkeeper	Accountant
Authorising the purchase of a new printer		
Coding the printer invoice		
Entering the printer invoice into the computer		
Authorising payment of the printer invoice		

✎ Test your understanding 3

Why is it important Jessica and other accounting professionals to continually develop their skills?

1.6   Ethical behaviour

Behaving ethically means doing the right thing at the right time. Accounting professionals are trusted by their employers to handle confidential and sensitive information in an appropriate manner.

The AAT has published a set of ethical guidelines to follow – see www.aatethics.org.uk/code/. These fundamental principles form part of the guidelines:

- **Confidentiality** – as described later in this chapter, it is important that information is not disclosed to third parties, used for personal gain or shared unless there is a legal or professional duty to do so.

- **Objectivity** – accountants should remain independent and show sound judgement rather than allowing bias, personal interests or pressure from others to influence them.

- **Integrity** - being straightforward and honest when you perform your duties.

- **Professional behaviour and competence** – being able to perform your job to an acceptable level and provide a good service. All accounting professionals should undergo regular training to keep their technical knowledge up-to-date.

Test your understanding 4

In each of the following situations decide whether this is an example of ethical behaviour or not. For each, state which ethical principle is being considered.	Is this ethical behaviour?		Which ethical principle is being considered?
	Yes	No	
Discussing the issues one of your clients is facing when with your friends over dinner.			
Providing advice on an area of tax accounting you are not familiar with to a customer.			
Completing the accounts on time and bearing in mind all recent changes in legislation.			
Changing the contents of a report because your manager offered you a financial bonus to do so.			

Test your understanding 5

Which of the following are principles that a professional accountant should follow in order to demonstrate ethical behaviour?

Tick ALL that apply.

	✓
Confidentiality	
Flexibility	
Integrity	
Confidence	
Numeracy	

2 Confidentiality and data security

2.1 Confidentiality

Information that is being processed by a bookkeeper will be both sensitive and/or private. Whether the information is held on paper or held electronically on a computer, a bookkeeper must make sure that confidential information is kept in a safe and secure way. This will help to prevent loss and the unauthorised sharing of information.

2.2 Commercial information

Information held by the accounts department or being processed by a bookkeeper may be commercially sensitive. For example, the price paid for a particular product, or discounts given to customers. If a competitor of the business knew this information they might be able to use it as a competitive advantage. It is therefore imperative to protect customer information and to only share information with authorised personnel, otherwise this could be damaging to the business.

2.3 Personal information

Personal information held about individuals, such as employees and customers, is protected by law. The Data Protection Act sets out rules about how personal data can be used.

The Act sets out eight data protection principles which must be followed when processing personal data.

The information must be:

1. used fairly and lawfully

2. used for limited, specifically stated purposes

3. used in a way that is adequate, relevant and not excessive

4. accurate

5. kept for no longer than is absolutely necessary

6. handled according to people's data protection rights

7. kept safe and secure

8. not transferred outside the European Economic Area without adequate protection

Any organisations who process personal data must register with the Information Commissioner's Office in order to be permitted to process data. The Information Commissioner's Office (ICO) is the UK's independent body set up to uphold information rights. You can find out how personal information is protected by visiting their website: https://www.ico.org.uk

Whether personal and sensitive information is held on computer or in a paper based filing system, it must be kept safe and secure. This means it must be kept away from any unauthorised access. It would be wrong to leave personal data open to be viewed by just anyone.

📝 **Test your understanding 6**

Tick the appropriate box for the statements provided:

Commercial information is information that can be sold to anyone, so it does not have to be kept confidential.

True ☐ or False ☐

You have finished working on a document, you have made notes on paper that you do not need anymore. Are you going to:

Discard the paper in the bin ☐   Shred the paper ☐

2.4   The security of confidential information

Advances in technology have enabled organisations to process more and more personal data, and to share information more easily. This has obvious benefits, but it also gives rise to equally obvious security risks.

If data is not properly safeguarded, this can seriously damage an organisation's reputation and compromise the safety of individuals.

If a bookkeeper is given sensitive information to work with, it is their responsibility to keep it safe and secure.

Below are some examples of how to keep confidential information secure in the role of a bookkeeper.

Example

Situation	Paper based filing system	Information held on a computer
Confidential information you are currently working with.	Any confidential information you are responsible for should be kept close by you at all times so that you are aware if anyone tries to read it. To avoid the information being seen by anyone passing by your desk, all confidential paperwork should be kept face down or in a folder until you need to work with it.	You may need to change the position of your computer screen to make sure that unauthorised people cannot see information on your computer screen as you are working. If this is not possible, you may need to move desks or offices to ensure that you can carry out the work. Sensitive information held on computers should be protected by multi-level passwords so that employees only see what is relevant to them. Never share your password with unauthorised people.
If you have to leave your workstation	If you have to leave your desk always put any confidential papers in a locked drawer or filing cabinet.	You should use the screen lock on your computer so that confidential information cannot be read by people passing your desk when you are away.
Storage of confidential information	Sensitive information should be kept in a locked filing cabinet, until it is needed.	Regular back-ups of computer data should be taken and stored in fireproof cabinets.
Out of date information	When confidential information is no longer needed it should be shredded before being recycled.	Data should be removed or deleted from computers by authorised staff from the Information Technology (IT) department.

Definition

Authorised person – Someone who has been given permission to do something on somebody else's behalf. For example, an employee who has been authorised to input confidential information onto a computer.

2.5   Passwords

As a bookkeeper, you will have many passwords for different systems and processes. For example, you will have a password to be able to gain access to the computer system itself, you will then need another password to gain access to the accounting software and the chances are that other documents will be password protected for you to be able to view them.

It is important that you keep your password safe and secure and change it regularly in line with the company procedures or immediately if you suspect that someone has found out what your password is. You should avoid the use of names or dates that are personal to you as quite often these can be easy to guess. Ideally you should create a password that contains both upper and lower case letters, numbers and symbols. The harder it is for someone to guess your password, the harder it is for them to access sensitive information.

✎ Test your understanding 7

You have recently set up online banking for your current account.

You need to set a password for access to the online banking facilities. Which of the following would make a good password? Tick the TWO best answers from the options given.

	✓
Something you cannot remember	
Something other people are not likely to know	
Something obvious	
The word 'password'	
Your name and year of birth	
A combination of letters, numbers and symbols	
Something you saved on your PC in a file called Passwords	

🖉 Test your understanding 8

Below is a list of statements. State which are true and which are false.

Statement	True/False
Passwords can be shared with colleagues who are doing the same type work.	
All cabinet drawers with personal or commercial information in should be kept locked.	
If leaving your work station, you must ensure that the screen is blank and computer access blocked.	

2.6 Backups

It is important that regular backups are taken of the data within an organisation. Usually a company will take a backup of the information held on their server at least once a day. There should be more than one copy of the back up in case one of them becomes corrupt. A copy of the backup data should be kept in a fireproof cabinet or taken of site in case of an unexpected disaster such as a fire or a flood.

2.7 Anti-virus software

Anti-virus software is another key way in which an organisation can keep confidential information safe and secure. This is a piece of software that is installed onto the computer system which will then scan information such as emails for viruses and will block any content that appears suspect. Viruses can be extremely dangerous as they can shut down a whole system in a very short space of time. If data becomes corrupt, you will not be able to see or use it therefore it is very important that an organisation protects itself with anti-virus software.

🖉 Test your understanding 9

You have been working on a confidential document on your computer and have to leave the office for ten minutes to deal with a customer. How can you keep the information on your screen confidential?

	✓
Switch the computer off	
Use the screen lock facility to lock the computer screen	
Stay at your desk	
Put some papers over the screen to hide the information	

Test your understanding 10

Complete the following sentences:

a) I need to go to the bathroom, I should use my computer _____ lock.

b) I have finished with this confidential paper so I am going to _____ it.

c) I don't want anyone to read this paperwork so I am going to put it _____ on my desk.

d) _____ software is another way of keeping information safe and secure.

e) Backed up computer data should be stored in _____ cabinets.

3 Summary and further questions

In this chapter we have described the role of a bookkeeper. You should now know that bookkeepers prepare and check financial documents and transactions to be authorised by an accountant.

You should also understand the importance of keeping information confidential and know different methods of doing this and recognise the importance of working in an ethical manner and how this helps to protect the bookkeeping data.

Let us return to our case study to see how Jessica applies this knowledge.

Case study activity 1

Jessica is asked to attend a staff meeting at How Two Ltd. Otto, the Sales Manager, asks Jessica what her role as a bookkeeper for the company entails.

Which TWO of the following answers would be the most appropriate?

	✓
Analysing the financial performance of the business	
Advising the Managing Director	
Recording and checking financial transactions	
Processing documents such as sales invoices as required	
Deciding pay increases	
Saving costs for the business	

Case study activity 2

Jessica is aware that there are many departments for which the accounting team at How Two Ltd provide information.

Match the department with the correct definition.

Department	Definition
PRODUCTION	This department sells the company's goods and services to customers.
SALES	This department is responsible for typing, collecting and distributing mail, keeping & filing records, organising meetings and maintaining resources.
ADMINISTRATION	This department deals with the recruitment of new staff, the training of new and existing staff, pay negotiations and regular staff appraisals.
ACCOUNTING	This department is responsible for producing the goods or services that a business provides by making best use of the various inputs.
HUMAN RESOURCES	This department is responsible for keeping records and accounts, for giving advice on budgets to other departments, and for paying wages and salaries.

Case study activity 3

Jessica has been asked to create her own unique password for the accounting system.

Which of the following passwords should she use?

a)   Password123

b)   JHoward011200

c)   JessHowTw0

d)   4yXkj2fR!*

📖 Case study activity 4

During a conversation in the staff canteen, several members of staff were discussing their rates of pay and the company bonus.

One of them, Neelam is upset that other people are being paid more than her. She asks Jessica to find out for her if one of her colleagues, Jason, is indeed being paid more than her.

What reply should Jessica give?

Statement	Correct?
Jessica confirms the amount that Jason does indeed receive more money than Neelam.	
Jessica tells Neelam that she will speak to her manager to see if she can tell her the information.	
Jessica explains to Neelam that this information is confidential and cannot be disclosed.	
Jessica ensures that all pay rates are accessible to all employees to avoid any future debate.	

Answers to chapter activities

📝 Test your understanding 1

Fill in the gaps from the pick list below to complete the paragraph about bookkeepers.

The bookkeeper is responsible for **inputting** the financial **transactions** of an organisation. An accountant is responsible for **interpreting** the financial **information** of an organisation.

The **Accountant** suggests alternative strategies, based on the interpretation of the financial information. The **manager** will make the decisions.

A bookkeeper may start as a **bookkeeper**, but, with hard work and study, can progress to **senior** accountant.

📝 Test your understanding 2

Role	Bookkeeper	Accountant
Authorising the purchase of a new printer		✔
Coding the printer invoice	✔	
Entering the printer invoice into the computer	✔	
Authorising payment of the printer invoice		✔

📝 Test your understanding 3

Jessica and all bookkeepers and accounting professionals need to ensure that they remain competent for the work they do.

To do so, they will need to keep up to date with changing regulations that affect their work.

They will also need to keep up to date with technologies that help them do their work efficiently and effectively.

Test your understanding 4

	Ethical?		Ethical principle
	Yes	No	
Discussing the issues one of your clients is facing when with your friends over dinner.		✔	Confidentiality
Providing advice on an area of tax accounting you are not familiar with to a customer.		✔	Integrity
Completing the accounts on time and bearing in mind all recent changes in legislation.	✔		Professional behaviour & competence
Changing the contents of a report because your manager offered you a financial bonus to do so.		✔	Objectivity

Test your understanding 5

	✔
Confidentiality	✔
Flexibility	
Integrity	✔
Confidence	
Numeracy	

Test your understanding 6

Commercial information is information that can be sold to anyone, so it does not have to be kept confidential.

True ☐ or False ✔

You have finished working on a document, you have made notes on paper that you do not need anymore. Are you going to:

Discard the paper in the bin ☐   Shred the paper ✔

Test your understanding 7

	✓
Something you cannot remember	
Something other people are not likely to know	✓
Something obvious	
The word 'password'	
Your name and year of birth	
A combination of letters, numbers and symbols	✓
Something you saved on your PC in a file called Passwords	

Test your understanding 8

Statement	True/False
Passwords can be shared with colleagues who are doing the same type work.	False
All cabinet drawers with personal or commercial information in should be kept locked.	True
If leaving your work station, you must ensure that the screen is blank and computer access blocked.	True

Test your understanding 9

	✓
Switch the computer off	
Use the screen lock facility to lock the computer screen	✓
Stay at your desk	
Put some papers over the screen to hide the information	

Test your understanding 10

a) I need to go to the bathroom, I should use my computer **screen lock**.

b) I have finished with this confidential paper so I am going to **shred** it.

c) I don't want anyone to read this paperwork so I am going to put it **face down** on my desk.

d) **Anti-virus** software is another way of keeping information safe and secure.

e) Backed up computer data should be stored in **fireproof** cabinets.

Case study activity 1

	✓
Analysing the financial performance of the business	
Advising the Managing Director	
Recording and checking financial transactions	✓
Processing documents such as sales invoices as required	✓
Deciding pay increases	
Saving costs for the business	

Case study activity 2

Department	Definition
PRODUCTION	This department is responsible for producing the goods or services that a business provides by making best use of the various inputs.
SALES	This department sells the company's goods and services to customers.
ADMINISTRATION	This department is responsible for typing, collecting and distributing mail, keeping & filing records, organising meetings and maintaining resources.
ACCOUNTING	This department is responsible for keeping records and accounts, for giving advice on budgets to other departments, and for paying wages and salaries.
HUMAN RESOURCES	This department deals with the recruitment of new staff, the training of new and existing staff, pay negotiations and regular staff appraisals.

Case study activity 3

She should use:

d)   4yXkj2fR!*

Case study activity 4

Statement	Correct?
Jessica confirms the amount that Jason does indeed receive more money than Neelam.	
Jessica tells Neelam that she will speak to her manager to see if she can tell her the information.	
Jessica explains to Neelam that this information is confidential and cannot be disclosed.	✓
Jessica ensures that all pay rates are accessible to all employees to avoid any future debate.	

Bookkeeping terminology

2

Introduction

The purpose of accounting is to be able to provide financial information about an organisation. For example, managers will want to keep track of the profit made by the organisation in a certain period, and they will also want to see how much the organisation is worth at a specific point in time.

To be able to provide this information it is important to understand the principles of sales and purchases and how these contribute to the profit or loss of a company.

This chapter will introduce you to the accounting terminology used in relation to this.

KNOWLEDGE	CONTENTS
Understand financial transactions	1 Assets and liabilities
2.1 The buying and selling process	2 Income and expenditure
2.2 Basic bookkeeping terminology	3 Cash and credit transactions
	4 Profit and loss
	5 Summary and further questions

1 Assets and liabilities

1.1 Case study: an introduction

📖 Case study

Having established the importance of accuracy and confidentiality, Jessica is now more aware of what a career in bookkeeping entails.

She now needs to understand some of the key words and concepts she will encounter during her apprenticeship at How Two Ltd. To be effective, Jessica will need to grasp the principles of sales and purchasing and identify how they can assist a business to generate more income by means of saving on expenditure. Jessica therefore needs to use the correct terminology for each task so it will help her when it comes to completing her work, as well as when she takes her accountancy exams moving forward.

Jessica also wants to gain a greater understanding of the effect expenditure and income has on profit/loss. She finds that practising activities helps to understand these concepts.

1.2 What is an asset?

Assets are items of value which an organisation owns in order to generate profit by selling goods or providing a service.

Assets can be physical such as cash, land, buildings etc. or non-physical such as copyrights, trademarks and patents. Either way, an asset is something that a company acquires to help increase its value or to improve its overall operations.

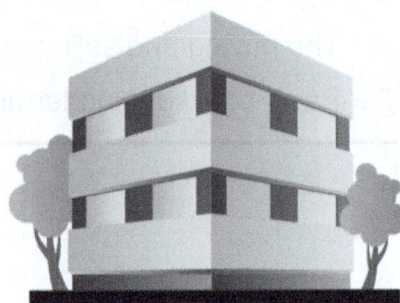

🔍 Definition

An asset is an item of value owned by an organisation.

1.3 Different types of asset

> ### 💡 Examples
>
> Assets include:
>
> **Premises** – organisations usually need a building from which to carry out their business. These premises could be an office building, a shop, or a factory.
>
> **Fixtures and fittings** – these are items in the premises which are used to provide goods or services. For example, the computers in an office, the shelving in a shop, or machinery in a factory.
>
> **Vehicles** – vehicles may be needed to deliver goods or provide a service to customers.
>
> **Inventory** – goods which are ready to sell to customers are kept in stock
>
> **Bank** – the funds available in the organisation's bank account may be used to purchase more stock to sell.
>
> **Cash** – some organisations keep money on the premises so that they can buy small items.
>
> **Trade Receivables** – amounts owed to the organisation by customers as a result of sales made on credit.
>
> **Copyrights** – a legal right which protects any work created by an organisation. It prevents others from using it or distributing it without their permission
>
> **Trademarks** – the brand, logo or slogan of an organisation which helps to distinguish it from another organisation. For example, Tesco is a 'brand'. Nobody would be allowed to set up a shop of their own and call it Tesco, as the name belongs to them.
>
> **Patents** – if an organisation invents a new product, they may apply for a patent from the government which stops others for a limited period of time from creating, using or selling it without their permission.

1.4 What is a liability?

A liability is an amount of money that an organisation owes to a supplier, bank or other lender. An organisation will have a legal obligation to pay back the money that they owe. The money will usually have been used to buy assets for the organisation to use.

Total liabilities are deducted from total assets to calculate an organisation's worth at a specific period in time.

Definition

A liability is a debt owed by an organisation to other organisations, businesses and individuals.

1.5   Different types of liability

Examples

Liabilities include:

Payables – amounts owed by the organisation to suppliers of goods and services.

Bank Overdraft – an arrangement that allows an organisation to take more money out of its bank than it has put in. The money is owed to the bank on a short-term basis.

Bank Loan – a fixed amount of money an organisation borrows from the bank usually over a longer period of time.

Test your understanding 1

Jessica had to classify the following as an asset or a liability to be able to identify them accurately within the system.

Classify them accurately by putting a tick in the correct box.

	Asset	Liability
Machinery		
A bank loan		
A bank overdraft		
Inventory		
Receivables		
Payables		
A patent		

2 Income and expenditure

2.1 Introduction

The purpose of most organisations is to make a profit or to raise funds so that they can continue supplying goods and services to customers. To calculate profit, **expenditure** is deducted from **income**.

2.2 What is income?

Any money received from the supply of goods and services to customers is known as income.

2.3 What is expenditure?

Any money paid for purchasing the goods and services and day to day expenses is known as expenditure.

🔍 Definitions

Income is the money received by an organisation from selling its goods and services.

Expenditure is the money paid by an organisation to purchase goods and services.

📝 Test your understanding 2

Jessica needs to classify the following as income or expenditure to be able to identify them accurately within the system. Classify them accurately by putting a tick in the correct box.

	Income	Expenditure
Payments to suppliers		
Electricity bill		
The cost of goods and services		
Cash sales		
Sales of services		
Telephone bill		
Water bill		

---

3 Cash and credit transactions

3.1 Recording cash and credit transactions

Income is the amount of money received by an organisation from the sale of its goods or services. Returning to our case study, How Two Ltd sell computers and accessories to their customers; these would be classified as their sales of goods. They also have a help desk that offer advice on technical issues or who deal with broken computers that customers bring into store to be fixed; this would be classified as their sales of services.

Income is the amount of money received by an organisation from its sales. Sometimes the money is received immediately, this is called a **cash sale.** Sometimes the money is received later, this is called a **credit sale**. It is important that cash and credit transactions are recorded separately so that the organisation knows how much money it is owed by customers, and how much it owes to suppliers.

3.2 Cash and credit sales

Definitions

Sales is the exchange of goods or services to an individual or organisation in exchange for money.

A **customer** is an individual or organisation to whom the goods or services have been sold. The organisation supplying the goods or services will then receive money in exchange.

A **trade receivable (also known as a debtor)** is a customer who has been sold goods on credit and who owes the business the money in respect of the sale.

Cash Sales is the term used to describe a payment at point of sale. The payment itself can be made by cash (currency), cheque, debit or credit card, or bank transfer. An example of a cash sale is when you go into a shop, choose the items you want to buy, and pay for them immediately.

Credit Sales are sales made where the goods or services will be paid later than the point of sale. Many organisations give credit to their regular trade customers so that one payment can be made for all the transactions made in each month. Credit sales are usually recorded by way of an invoice which will be covered in a later chapter.

3.3 Cash and credit customers

With cash sales the organisation gets the money immediately from the customer and the relationship ends there. With credit customers, there is a risk to the organisation that the customer may not pay for the goods.

Therefore, before allowing customers to pay on credit the organisation will make certain checks to ensure that the customer can pay. If these checks identify that the customer has the ability to pay its debts, payment terms will be agreed with the customer and a credit account set up.

Payment terms usually state the length of time a customer has to pay for their goods and also a maximum amount that they are allowed to owe the business at any one time. The amounts outstanding from customers can be analysed so that a business can see at what point they can expect the money to come into their bank account.

If customers are taking longer to pay than expected, a business should chase for the outstanding monies to ensure a continual flow of cash moving through the organisation.

It is assumed that the money owed by credit customers will be paid and therefore they are classed as **trade receivables or receivables**. Receivables have the ability to be converted into cash and are therefore classed as assets of the organisation.

Test your understanding 3

Jessica has been asked to identify whether the following How Two Ltd transactions would be classified as a cash or credit transaction?

Put a tick in the correct box.

	Cash	Credit
A customer purchases a computer and pays by credit card		
A customer buys a mouse mat, a mouse and a printer and pays by debit card		
A customer buys 5 tablet computers, and pays in 30 days		

3.4   Cash and credit purchases

> ### 🔍 Definition
>
> **Purchases** – to buy goods or services from an organisation in exchange for money.

Cash Purchases are when goods or services are paid for at the time of purchase.

> ### 📖 Case study
>
> How Two Ltd may purchase some stock and pay by 'cash'. Although the payment could be by cash (currency), credit card or debit card or bank transfer, if the payment is made immediately it is classed as a cash purchase.

Credit Purchases are when an organisation pays for the goods or services sometime after making the purchase. The money will be sent to the supplier after an agreed amount of time, for example, thirty days.

The supplier is now a payable of the organisation and as money is owed to the supplier in respect of the transaction, they are classed as a liability of the business.

> ### 🔍 Definition
>
> A **supplier** is an individual or organisation providing goods or services to another in exchange for money.
>
> A **trade payable** is a supplier who is owed money for goods purchased on credit.

> ### ✏️ Test your understanding 4
>
> Fill in the gaps below to complete the sentences. Choose from the Pick list provided.
>
> When an organisation pays for items of expenditure at the time of purchase this is known as a _____
>
> When an organisation allows a customer to pay the amount they owe at a later date this is known as a _____
>
> **Pick List**
>
> credit sale   cash sale   cash purchase   credit purchase.

Test your understanding 5

Match the definition with the correct term.

Terms	Definition
Payable	Something the business owns
Receivable	A person or another business that the organisation owes money to
Asset	Something the business owes
Liability	A person or another business that owes money to the organisation

Test your understanding 6

Jessica has been asked to identify whether the following How Two Ltd transactions would be classified as a cash or credit transaction?

Put a tick in the correct box.

	Cash	Credit
The Liverpool office purchases some inventory online and pays by bank transfer		
The London office purchases some inventory and is issued an invoice from the supplier		
The Manchester office purchases a computer and pays by credit card		

Test your understanding 7

C Froome's Cycle World

Mr Froome has a small shop selling and repairing bicycles for individual customers.

He buys the spare parts that he needs from a large wholesaler.

Do you think that Mr Froome's income comes from cash sales or credit sales?

Do you think that the expenditure for spare parts is cash purchases or credit purchases?

3.5   The Cash Book and Petty Cash Book

The word 'cash' is also used in accounting as a name for recording monetary transactions.

A **Cash Book** is used to keep a record of most of the receipts of income and payments of expenses made by the organisation. The actual monies received and recorded may be by cash (currency), cheque, credit card or debit card, or bank transfer.

A **Petty Cash Book** is used to record small amounts of cash that most businesses hold in order to make small cash payments regularly. Petty cash systems and the management of petty cash are addressed further, later in this book.

4   Profit and loss

4.1   What is a profit or loss?

A business needs to make money in order to operate. By selling goods or services they generate income, from this they need to deduct their expenses for buying in those goods and services. This is called the 'profit' or 'loss'.

In order for a business to generate a 'profit', their income needs to be more than their expenses. If their expenses are more than their income, they would make a loss which could make the business fail.

Definitions

Profit is the amount of money an organisation earns after expenditure has been deducted from income.

Loss is when an organisation has spent more money than it has earned from income.

4.2 What happens when a business makes a profit?

An organisation's main goal should be to make a profit. No business can survive long-term if they don't make a profit.

Profit is paid to the owners of a company or its shareholders. Alternatively, it can be used as a saving opportunity to enable the organisation to re-invest and therefore grow the business. Growing a business means expanding it; making it bigger. This may be through investing in research or new technology, opening new offices, operating in new markets or obtaining other businesses. A bigger company means a bigger part of the market share and therefore increased profitability.

4.3 What happens when a business makes a loss?

If a business is spending more on expenses than they are making from the sales of goods or services, they will be making a loss.

If an organisation is making a loss then the chances are that their bank account may become overdrawn. Ultimately, they will be charged high amounts of interest for this which only increases their expenditure even more. If this were to happen, the business may not have enough money to pay their suppliers which could result in the suppliers putting their account on hold, or even withdrawing their credit agreement.

As a result, the business would find it difficult to purchase goods or services for resale, meaning that they would struggle to meet their customer's demands. If this is the case, it can cause problems and the business could fail.

Test your understanding 8

Jessica has been asked to identify which of the following are indicators of a business making a profit or a loss. Put a tick in the correct box.

	Profit	Loss
The business could fail		
The bank account is overdrawn		
A saving opportunity		
There is an opportunity for growth		
There is a high volume of sales		
Money has been invested in new ventures		
Not enough money to pay for purchases		
Suppliers withdraw their credit agreement		

Example

NB Solutions Ltd has recorded all sales income and expenditure for the previous month. Alba, the Accounts Assistant, has been asked to calculate the profit for the month.

	£
Sales income	125,000
Cost of sales	75,000
Wages	15,000
Premises expenses	3,000
Vehicle expenses	2,500

Solution:

To calculate **profit (or loss)** the cost of sales are deducted from the sales income.

	Sales income:	£125,000
–	Cost of sales	- £75,000
–	Wages	- £15,000
–	Premises expenses	- £3,000
–	Vehicle expenses	- £2,500
=	**Total Profit**	**£29,500**

Therefore, Alba can report a profit of £29,500 for the month.

Note: If Alba had ended up with a minus figure at the end of her calculation, she would know that the company had made a loss i.e. NB Solutions Ltd's expenses were more than the company's income.

Case study

In September, How Two Ltd's Liverpool office had recorded income from sales of £82,000. The cost of those sales was £66,000 and the other expenses were £25,000. Jessica is asked whether the Liverpool office made a profit or a loss.

Solution:

	Sales income:	£82,000
–	Cost of sales	- £66,000
–	Other expenses	- £25,000
=		**-£9,000**

Their expenses are more than their income so the Liverpool office of How Two Ltd made a loss of £9,000 in September.

Test your understanding 9

To assess the performance of How Two Ltd's Liverpool office in September, Jessica looks at the figures from the previous month. In August, the Liverpool office recorded income of £85,000. The cost of those sales was £69,000 and the other expenses were £18,000.

Did they make a profit or a loss? How do the two months compare?

Test your understanding 10

Jessica has been asked to see if the performance of the Liverpool office is similar to the nearest office, in Manchester. The Manchester office of How Two Ltd has recorded all sales income and expenditure for the previous month.

Jessica needs to calculate the profit or loss for the month given the following information:

	£
Sales income from cash and credit sales	78,000
Cost of sales	50,700
Wages	7,500
Premises expenses	1,750
Vehicle expenses	2,000

Test your understanding 11

Jessica concludes that in some cases, How Two Ltd offices have total income lower than costs of sales plus expenses.

Jessica must look at this statement and then determine – have these offices made a profit or a loss? She must provide a brief explanation for her answer for one of the departmental managers.

5 Summary and further questions

This chapter has introduced you to some important accounting terminology. You can distinguish between assets, liabilities, income and expenditure and looked at the difference between credit sales and purchases and cash sales and purchases.

Finally, the chapter looked at how the profit or loss of an organisation is calculated and you should understand that a business needs more income than expenses in order to operate profitably.

Let us now return to the case study for some further practice questions to test your knowledge of this key terminology.

📖 Case study activity 5

Jessica has been asked to define some key terms to help explain her e-mail to the managers. Choose the correct option in each statement:

a. The sum of money spent in making sales is known as [sales/cost of sales]

b. If total income is greater than the cost of sales plus other expenses the organisation has made a [profit/loss]

c. If total income is less than the cost of sales plus other expenses the organisation has made a [profit/loss]

📖 Case study activity 6

Jessica has been given a list of terms which are commonly used every day in her department. She needs to decide if they are assets, liabilities, income or expenditure? Put a tick in the correct box.

	Asset	Liability	Income	Expenditure
Creditors				
Electricity bill				
Money in the bank				
Bank overdraft				
Sales to customers				
Debtors				
Office computers				

KAPLAN PUBLISHING

Case study activity 7

Jessica needs to decide whether the following How Two Ltd transactions are cash or credit sales, or cash or credit purchases? Put a tick in the correct box.

	Cash Sale	Credit Sale	Cash Purchase	Credit Purchase
Printer paper bought from a supplier and paid for immediately.				
Cables delivered to a customer who will pay at the end of the month.				
Laptop components bought from a supplier on credit.				
A payment received from a customer for goods purchased online and paid for at the checkout.				

Case study activity 8

Last month How Two Ltd's Head Office recorded income and expenditure in the table below:

Income and Expenditure	£
Sales	156,000
Cost of Sales	93,600
Wages	21,060
Administration Expenses	18,720
Selling Expenses	12,844

Jessica needs to use the income and expenditure figures to calculate the profit or loss and state underneath whether this would be a profit or loss.

Profit / Loss: £

📖 **Case study activity 9**

The following month's recorded income and expenditure is shown in the table below:

Income and Expenditure	£
Sales	152,880
Cost of Sales	91,728
Wages	20,640
Administration Expenses	18,350
Selling Expenses	12,590

Jessica needs to use the income and expenditure figures to calculate the profit or loss and state underneath whether this would be a profit or loss.

Profit / Loss: £

Answers to chapter activities

Test your understanding 1

	Asset	Liability
Machinery	✓	
A bank loan		✓
A bank overdraft		✓
Inventory	✓	
Receivables	✓	
Payables		✓
A patent	✓	

Test your understanding 2

	Income	Expenditure
Payments to suppliers		✓
Electricity bill		✓
The cost of goods and services		✓
Cash sales	✓	
Sales of services	✓	
Telephone bill		✓
Water bill		✓

Test your understanding 3

	Cash	Credit
A customer purchases a computer and pays by credit card	✓	
A customer buys a mouse mat, a mouse and a printer and pays by debit card	✓	
A customer buys 5 tablet computers, and pays in 30 days		✓

Test your understanding 4

When an organisation pays for items of expenditure at the time of purchase this is known as a **cash purchase.**

When an organisation allows a customer to pay the amount they owe at a later date this is known as a **credit sale.**

Test your understanding 5

Terms	Definition
Payable	Something the business owns
Receivable	A person or another business that the organisation owes money to
Asset	Something the business owes
Liability	A person or another business that owes money to the organisation

Payable → A person or another business that the organisation owes money to
Receivable → A person or another business that owes money to the organisation
Asset → Something the business owns
Liability → Something the business owes

Test your understanding 6

	Cash	Credit
The Liverpool office purchases some inventory online and pays by bank transfer	✓	
The London office purchases some inventory and is issued an invoice from the supplier		✓
The Manchester office purchases a computer and pays by credit card	✓	

KAPLAN PUBLISHING

Test your understanding 7

Mr Froome's income is most likely to be from cash sales. His customers are individuals who will probably pay when they come to pick up their bicycles. They are unlikely to be very regular customers.

His expenditure for the spare parts is likely to be a credit purchase. As Mr Froome will buy regularly from the supplier he may have been given credit so that he can make daily or weekly purchases and then pay for all he owes at a later date.

Test your understanding 8

	Profit	Loss
The business could fail		✓
The bank account is overdrawn		✓
A saving opportunity	✓	
There is an opportunity for growth	✓	
There is a high volume of sales	✓	
Money has been invested in new ventures	✓	
Not enough money to pay for purchases		✓
Suppliers withdraw their credit agreement		✓

Test your understanding 9

	£
Sales income	85,000
Cost of sales	-69,000
Other expenses	-18,000
	-2,000

This means that their sales income is lower than their expenses and therefore they have made **a loss of £2,000**.

Although this is a loss, it is £7,000 less than the loss in September.

Test your understanding 10

	£
Sales income	78,000
Cost of sales	-50,700
Wages	-7,500
Premises expenses	-1,750
Vehicle expenses	-2,000
	16,050

The company have made **a profit of £16,050** because their sales income is more than the total of their expenditure.

Test your understanding 11

As their sales income is lower than cost of sales plus expenses, the business has made a loss.

Case study activity 5

a. The sum of money spent in making sales is known as **cost of sales**
b. If total income is greater than the cost of sales plus other expenses the organisation has made a **profit**
c. If total income is less than the cost of sales plus other expenses the organisation has made a **loss**

Case study activity 6

	Asset	Liability	Income	Expenditure
Creditors		✓		
Electricity bill				✓
Money in the bank	✓			
Bank overdraft		✓		
Sales to customers			✓	
Debtors	✓			
Office computers	✓			

Case study activity 7

	Cash Sale	Credit Sale	Cash Purchase	Credit Purchase
Printer paper bought from a supplier and paid for immediately.			✓	
Cables delivered to a customer who will pay at the end of the month.		✓		
Laptop components bought from a supplier on credit.				✓
A payment received from a customer for goods purchased online and paid for at the checkout.	✓			

Case study activity 8

	£
Sales	156,000
Cost of Sales	-93,600
Wages	-21,060
Administration Expenses	-18,720
Selling Expenses	-12,844
	9,776

Profit / Loss: £ 9,776 Profit

Case study activity 9

	£
Sales	152,880
Cost of Sales	-91,728
Wages	-20,640
Administration Expenses	-18,350
Selling Expenses	-12,590
	9,572

Profit / Loss: £9,572 Profit

Business documentation

3

Introduction

It is important that customer and supplier transactions are recorded separately so that organisations know how much money they are owed by customers, and how much they owe to suppliers.

Business documents are used to record these transactions and the documents are exchanged between the supplier and the customer so that both parties have a record of each transaction. It is important that both the supplier and the customer keep a copy of each of these documents. Mistakes can happen and each document is proof of each stage of the transaction.

The name of a document will depend on whether we look at it from the point of view of the seller or the purchaser. Thus an invoice may be called a 'sales invoice' for the seller but a 'purchase invoice' for the purchaser, although it is the same document.

KNOWLEDGE	CONTENTS
Understand financial transactions	1 Sales documentation
2.1 The buying and selling process	2 Purchases documentation
Process customer and supplier transactions	3 Summary and further questions
3.1 Prepare sales invoices and credit notes	
3.4 Identify outstanding amounts for individual customers and suppliers	

1 Sales documentation

1.1 Case study: an introduction

📖 Case study

Jessica knows that the purpose of accounting is to be able to provide financial information about an organisation and she understands the principles behind sales and purchases. She has now been tasked with looking through the different types of business documentation that she will come across on a day to day basis.

She needs to establish what information is required on each document and then she will then be given the opportunity of completing some of these herself to be checked by her manager.

Jessica also needs to demonstrate an understanding of the importance of working with accuracy when creating these documents and the impact that this has on the organisation if they are not completed correctly.

1.2 Offering credit and price quotations

Most transactions between business organisations will be on credit terms and this involves an element of risk. The goods are being taken away or delivered to the customer now with the promise of payment in the future. Therefore, suppliers must be confident that payment will be received.

In some organisations it is common practice to quote prices to customers over the telephone particularly if there is a catalogue or price list from which there are no deviations in price. However, some businesses will be prepared to offer certain customers goods at different prices and discounts may be offered and/or given to customers. Therefore, it is often the case that a price quotation is sent to a customer showing the price at which the goods that they want can be bought. The customer can then decide whether or not to buy the goods at that price. If they decide to purchase the goods upon receipt of the quotation, this can be used to generate the sales invoice later on in the sales process.

1.3 Purchase Order

If the customer is happy with the price quotation that they have received from the supplier then they will complete a purchase order for the goods or services required and send it to their supplier.

This document will state the details of the goods required, including:

- the quantity and description of the goods
- the price and other terms
- the supplier's code number for the items
- the date the order was placed.

When the supplier receives a purchase order, it is important for them to check all of the details carefully as it forms part of the sales contract.

- Is the price the same as the one which was quoted to the customer?
- Are the delivery terms acceptable?
- Are any discounts applicable?

📖 Case study

An example of a purchase order received by How Two Ltd:

PURCHASE ORDER

IT Geeks Ltd.
11 Mountjoy Street
LONDON W12 6RS
Tel: 0208 741 2962
Fax: 0208 741 2963
Date: 17 March 2017
Purchase order no: P01562

To:	Delivery address
How Two Ltd.	(if different from above)
1 Baker Street	Four Hills Hotel
London	Park Lane
WC1 8QT	London
	W1 1UY

Product	Ref	Quantity	Price per unit (excl. VAT) £	Total (excl. VAT) £
Dall Touchpad 2	DTD2	7	250.00	1750.00

Signed: **J Belle**
Purchasing Manager

Notes:

a) The customer, IT Geeks Ltd. has placed an order with the supplier of computers, How Two Ltd.

b) The purchase order clearly states that the customer wants to purchase 7 Dall Touch Pad 2's at a price of £250.00 each.

c) The total amount that the customer wants to pay for the tablet computers is £1,750.00 (7 touchpads x £250.00 = £1,750.00).

d) If How Two Ltd. do not agree with any of these details, they will need to contact IT Geeks Ltd. immediately. The purchase order has been signed by J Belle, the authorised signatory. This is important to demonstrate that the process has been completed as required by the business.

Definition

An **authorised signatory** is an individual who has been given permission to sign an official document on behalf of an organisation.

1.4   Delivery note

When the goods or services are supplied, the supplier will prepare a delivery note to give to the customer. This document will show:

- The name and contact details of the seller

- Name and contact details of the customer

- Date of issue

- Date of delivery of the goods

- Delivery note number

- Purchase order number

- A description of the goods contained in the order

- The quantity of each type of goods

The delivery note will be signed by the customer upon receipt of the goods or services, so that the supplier has proof that the customer received them. This also ensures that there is a clear audit trail in case of any later queries.

1.5 The sales invoice

After the goods have been delivered, the supplier will request payment from the customer by sending an invoice. The invoice will state the code, quantity, description and price of the goods. The invoice will also have a sequential number so that it can be filed in order. The documentation used in order to generate this would include the quotation if there is one, a price list if it's a standard invoice and the delivery note.

📖 **Case study**

An example of a sales invoice provided by How Two Ltd:

INVOICE

How Two Ltd.

1 Baker Street
London
WC1 8QT
Tel: 020 7890 1234
Fax: 020 7890 1235

Invoice no: 005673
Tax point: 25 March 2017
VAT reg no: 618 2201 63
Delivery note: DN00673
Account no: BEL65

To:	Delivery:	Delivery date:
IT Geeks Ltd.	Four Hills Hotel	25 March 2017
11 Mountjoy St	Park Lane	
London W12 6RS	London W1 1UY	
Date: 25 March 2017	**Sales order number:** 41161	

Product	Quantity	Price per unit (£)	Total (£)
Dall Touchpad 2	7	250.00	1,750.00
		VAT 20%	350.00
		Total	2,100.00
Payment terms: 14 days net			

Notes:

This invoice confirms the price of the goods supplied to the customer

a)   7 Dall Touchpad 2's which have been supplied to the IT Geeks Ltd.

b)   The price for the goods is £1,750.00

c)   Value Added Tax (VAT) of 20%, £350.00 has been added to the cost of the goods.

d)   The amount of £2,100.00 is now due from the customer.

e)   The payment is due in 14 days from the date of the invoice.

1.6   Pricing and discounts

Unit prices for goods or services are kept in master files which must be updated regularly. If a price quotation has been sent to a customer then this must be used to determine the price to use on the invoice.

Trade discounts are a definite amount that is deducted from the list price of the goods for the supplies to some customers, with the intention of encouraging and rewarding customer loyalty. As well as checking the actual calculation of the trade discount on the face of the invoice, the supplier's file or the price quotation should be checked to ensure that the correct percentage of trade discount has been deducted.

Even if no trade discount appears on the purchase invoice, the supplier's file or price quotation must still be checked as it may be that a trade discount should have been deducted.

A **bulk discount** is similar to a trade discount in that it is deducted from the list price on the invoice. However, a bulk discount is given by a supplier for orders above a certain size.

A **prompt payment discount** is offered to customers if they settle the invoice within a certain time period. The discount is expressed as a percentage of the invoice total but is not deducted from the invoice total as it is not certain whether or not it will be accepted. Instead the details of the settlement discount will be noted at the bottom of the invoice.

KAPLAN PUBLISHING

Test your understanding 1

Match the transaction to the relevant document:

Transaction	Document
A document sent by the supplier to the customer listing the goods or services supplied and requesting payment	Purchase Order
A document sent to a supplier detailing the goods that the customer wants to buy.	Invoice
A document sent to a customer to accompany the goods. The customer signs this upon receipt of their items.	Delivery Note

1.7 VAT (sales tax)

VAT (Value Added Tax) also known as Sales Tax, is collected on behalf of HMRC (Her Majesty's Revenue and Customs) by companies in the UK. VAT registered companies charge VAT on the supply of goods and services to their customers. They can claim back any VAT paid on their purchases. The amount that gets paid to HMRC is the total amount of VAT charged to their customers minus the total amount of VAT that they can claim back on their purchases.

Definitions

Sales tax (VAT) is charged on the **taxable supply of goods and services** in the United Kingdom by a **taxable person** in the course of a business carried on by him.

Output tax is the tax charged on the sale of goods and services.

Input tax is the tax paid on the purchase of goods and services.

1.8 Rates of VAT (sales tax)

Taxable supply is the supply of all items except those which are **exempt.** Examples of exempt items are as follows:

- certain land and buildings, where sold, leased or hired
- insurance
- postal services

Input tax cannot be reclaimed where the trader's supplies are all exempt.

There are three rates of sales tax (VAT in the UK) on taxable supplies:

1.   Some items are 'zero-rated' (similar to exempt except that input tax can be reclaimed), examples of which include:

- water and most types of food

- books and newspapers

- drugs and medicines

- children's clothing and footwear.

2.   There is a special rate of 5% for domestic fuel and power

3.   All other items are rated at the standard rate of 20%.

For the purpose of this assessment, you will normally be dealing with taxable supplies at the standard rate of 20%.

Therefore, if you are given the net price of goods, the price excluding VAT, then the amount of VAT is 20% or 20/100 of this price.

Note: VAT is always rounded down to the nearest penny.

Example

A sale is made for £360.48 plus VAT. What is the amount of VAT to be charged on this sale?

Solution

VAT = £360.48 × 20/100 = £72.09

Remember to round down to the nearest penny.

An alternative way of calculating this would to be to multiply the net amount of £360.48 by 20% = £72.09.

If a price is given that already includes the VAT then calculating the VAT requires an understanding of the price structure where VAT is concerned.

	%
Selling price excl. VAT (net)	100
VAT	20
	—
Selling price incl. VAT (gross)	120
	—

Example

How Two Ltd offer a small office starter pack, with a selling price of £3,000 **inclusive** of VAT. What is the VAT on the goods and the net price of these goods?

Solution

	£
Net price (£3,000 ÷ 120 x 100)	2,500
VAT (£3,000 ÷ 120 x 20)	500
	———
Gross price	3,000
	———

Test your understanding 2

Calculate the net, VAT and gross figures for the following transactions:

a)   A credit sale for £3,600 inclusive of VAT

b)   A cash sale for £2,800 exclusive of VAT

	a) Credit Sale	b) Cash Sale
Net		
VAT		
Gross		

Test your understanding 3

Alba works in the accounts office at NB Solutions Ltd. She has been asked to check three invoices relating to office supplies.

Invoice 1 – NB Solutions purchased 24 boxes of paper towels at £12.45 for each box. What is the total cost of the paper towels?

Invoice 2 – NB Solutions spent £250 excluding (or net of) VAT on stationery. How much VAT would be charged?

Invoice 3 – NB Solutions bought two new dishwashers for the staff kitchens, at a total cost of £480 including VAT. How much VAT would have been included in the cost?

1.9 Preparing a sales invoice

📖 **Case study**

As part of her role, Jessica deals with both sales and purchases.

How Two Ltd are a VAT registered IT and Computer Consumables company. Jessica prepares the sales invoices to be sent to the customer from the price list and a copy of the delivery note sent up to her by the sales department.

Today she has received the following delivery note from the sales department.

How Two Ltd.

Delivery note: 1036
Date of issue: 30th October 20X7
Purchase order number: PO1612

To: IT Crowd PLC.
19 Bond Street
Chichester
CH1 6MT

From: How Two Ltd.
1 Baker Street
London
WC1 8QT

Delivery Address:
As Above

Delivery date: 31st October 20X7

Quantity	Code	DESCRIPTION	Size
10	CJA 991	Codie Laptop	12"
15	CJA 992	Codie Laptop	14"
5	CJA 994	Codie Laptop	15.7"

Received by: ....

Signature: .... Date: ....

Code	Description	Screen Size	Unit price	VAT rate
CJA 991	Codie Laptop	12"	249.00	Standard
CJA 992	Codie Laptop	14"	279.00	Standard
CJA 993	Codie Laptop	15"	319.00	Standard
CJA 994	Codie Laptop	15.7"	349.00	Standard

The customer file shows that IT Crowd PLC's account number is ITC 4125 and that a trade discount of 10% is offered to this customer.

Jessica must now prepare the sales invoice. Today's date is 2nd November 20X7 and the last invoice issued was numbered 95123.

Solution

INVOICE

How Two Ltd.

Invoice to:
IT Crowd PLC.
19 Bond Street
Chichester
CH1 6MT

Deliver to:

As above

How Two Ltd
1 Baker Street
London
WC1 8QT

Tel: 0207 890 1234
Fax: 0207 890 1235

Invoice no: 95124
Tax point: 2nd November 17
VAT reg no: 618 2201 63
Delivery note no: 1036
Account no: ICT 4125

Code	Description	Quantity	VAT rate	Unit price	Amount net of VAT
			%	£	£
CJA 991	**Codie Laptop**	10	20	249.00	2,490.00
CJA 992	**Codie Laptop**	15	20	279.00	4,185.00
CJA 994	**Codie Laptop**	5	20	349.00	1,745.00
					8,420.00
Trade discount 10%					(842.00)
					7,578.00
VAT					1,515.60
Total amount payable					9,093.60

How did Jessica do it?

Step 1   Enter today's date on the invoice and the invoice number which should be the next number after the last sales invoice number.

Step 2   Enter the customer details – name, address and account number.

Step 3   Refer now to the delivery note copy and enter the delivery note number and the quantities, codes and descriptions of the goods.

Step 4   Refer to the price list and enter the unit prices of the goods and the rate of VAT

Step 5   Now for the calculations – firstly multiply the number of each item by the unit price to find the VAT exclusive price – then total these total prices – finally calculate the trade discount as 10% of this total, £8,420.00 × 10% = £842.00 and deduct it.

Step 6   Calculate the VAT – in this case there is only standard rate VAT on the laptops but you must remember to deduct the trade discount (£8,420 – £842) before calculating the VAT amount £7,578 × 20% = £1,515.60 – add the VAT to the invoice total after deducting the trade discount.

Test your understanding 4

As mentioned in the example above, as part of her role as a bookkeeper at How Two Ltd, Jessica is required to generate sales invoices.

Today she has received the following delivery note from the sales department.

Delivery Note

How Two Ltd.

To: St Peter's Secondary School
191 St. Petersgate
Manchester
M2 6KS

From: How Two Ltd.
1 Baker Street
London
WC1 8QT

Delivery Address:
As Above

Delivery note: 1114
Date of issue: 30th October 20X7
Purchase order number: P6486

Delivery date: 31st October 20X7

Quantity	Code	DESCRIPTION	Size
5	SMG 121	Samsong HD Monitor	17"
12	SMG 123	Samsong HD Monitor	24"
8	SMG 124	Samsong HD Monitor	28"

Received by: ....

Signature: .... Date: ....

Code	Description	Screen Size	Unit price	VAT rate
SMG 121	Samsong HD Monitor	17"	69.99	Standard
SMG 122	Samsong HD Monitor	19"	99.99	Standard
SMG 123	Samsong HD Monitor	24"	129.99	Standard
SMG 124	Samsong HD Monitor	28"	149.99	Standard

The customer file shows that St. Peter's Secondary School's account number is SPS 1124 and that a bulk discount of 15% is offered to this customer.

She must now prepare the sales invoice and pass it back to Dave Woody to be checked. Today's date is 3rd November 20X7 and the last invoice issued was numbered 95156.

Solution

INVOICE

How Two Ltd.

Invoice to:

How Two Ltd
1 Baker Street
London
WC1 8QT

Tel: 0207 890 1234
Fax: 0207 890 1235

Deliver to:

Invoice no:
Tax point:
VAT reg no:
Delivery note no:
Account no:

Code	Description	Quantity	VAT rate	Unit price	Amount net of VAT
			%	£	£
SMG 121					
SMG 123					
SMG 124					
Bulk discount					
VAT					
Total amount payable					

Test your understanding 5

You work for Cavalier Beds as a sales invoicing clerk. Your task is to prepare a sales invoice for each customer using the information below.

Today is 28 October, 20X6 and you have received the following delivery note from the sales department.

Use the information from the delivery note, the information from the customer file and the price list below to prepare an invoice for KP Furniture Ltd.

The last invoice issued was Invoice No. 67894.

Delivery Note:

Delivery note: 6785

To: KP Furniture Ltd
9 Paris Street
COLCHESTER
CF25 1XY

Cavalier Beds
3 Brussels Road
County Road
Gloucester
GL6 6TH
Tel: 01456 698271
Fax: 01456 698272

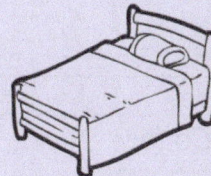

Delivery date: 27 October 20X6

Quantity	Code	DESCRIPTION	Size
5	MAT15K	Deluxe Mattress	King Size

Received by: ....

Signature: .... Date: ....

Customer File:

The customer file shows that KP Furniture Ltd's account number is KP12 and a trade discount of 10% is offered to this customer.

Price List:

Code	Description	Size	Unit price	VAT rate
MAT15S	Deluxe Mattress	Single	58.00	Standard
MAT15D	Deluxe Mattress	Double	74.00	Standard
MAT15K	Deluxe Mattress	King	98.00	Standard

Cavalier Beds
3 Brussels Road
County Road
Gloucester
GL6 6TH
Tel: 01456 698271   Fax: 01456 698272

Invoice to:

Invoice no:

Date:

VAT reg no: 488 7922 26

Delivery note no:

Account no:

Code		Quantity	VAT rate	Unit price £	Amount excl of VAT £
			20%	£	
Trade discount 10%					
Subtotal					
VAT					
Total amount payable					

1.9   Credit Notes

In some cases, the customer may want to return goods to the supplier. For example, if the goods are faulty. When this happens, the supplier will issue a credit note. This credit note will reduce the amount that the customer owes.

Common reasons for credit notes:

- when a customer has returned faulty or damaged goods
- when a customer has returned perfect goods by agreement with the supplier
- to make a refund for short deliveries
- to settle a dispute with a customer.

When a supplier receives returned goods they must be inspected, counted and recorded on receipt. They would normally be recorded on a goods returned note.

All credit notes must be authorised by a supervisor prior to being issued to the customer.

Some credit notes may be issued without a goods returned note. For example, an error may have been made in pricing on an invoice but the customer is satisfied with the goods and does not need to return them.

These credit notes must be issued only after written authorisation has been received and must be reviewed and approved before being sent to the customer or recorded.

As credit notes look very similar to invoices, they are often printed in red to make it clear that it is not an invoice.

📖 **Case study**

Credit Note

How Two Ltd.

1 Baker Street
London
WC1 8QT
Tel: 020 7890 1234
Fax: 020 7890 1235

Credit note no: CN 02542
Tax point: 30 November X7
VAT reg no: 618 2201 63
Invoice no: 95080
Account no: BEL65

CREDIT NOTE

Credit to:
Redshaw Cables
17 High Street
Manchester M1 6RS

Date: 30 November 2017

Description	Code	Quantity	Unit price £	Amount exclusive of VAT £
Epsan SXA Projector	ESXA14	1	300.00	300.00
VAT				60.00
Total amount of credit				360.00

Reason: Faulty

Notes

In this example, one of the Epsan SXA Projector's delivered to Redshaw Cables is faulty so they have requested a credit note.

When the replacement projector has been delivered, How Two Ltd. will raise another invoice for the replacement.

1.10 Remittance Advice

The final document in the process is the remittance advice. When the customer pays their outstanding balance, they will send a remittance advice to the supplier together with their payment.

The remittance advice will clearly show which invoices are being paid and the date of the payment.

If there are any credit notes, the customer will state which credit notes they are deducting from the payment.

Case study

REMITTANCE ADVICE

To:	Company name:	Redshaw Cables
How Two Ltd.		17 High Street
1 Baker Street	Address:	Manchester
London		M1 6RS
WC1 8QT		

VAT reg no: 32141108
Date: 5/12/20X7

Date	Your ref	Amount	Discount taken	Paid
		£	£	£
5/11/X7	Invoice 95080	2,160.00	0	2,160.00
30/11/X7	CN 02542	360.00	0	(360.00)

Total paid £1,800.00

Cheque no 041261

Notes

In this example, on 5th December 20X7, Redshaw Cables paid £1,800.00 by cheque. This payment is £2,160.00 for Invoice No 95080 less £360.00 for Credit Note CN02542.

If customers do not send a remittance advice and there are a lot of transactions in the month, it would be difficult for the supplier to know which invoices and credit notes the payment relates to.

2 Purchases

2.1 Payment terms

As mentioned previously, the majority of business transactions nowadays are conducted on credit terms. This applies to both sales and purchases.

When a credit account is set up with a supplier an agreement is put in place which states the point at which payment is to be made for goods and services, any conditions of payment and any discounts that may be applicable. This helps to ensure that suppliers are paid on time and to give them an idea of cash flows within the business i.e. at what point they can expect the money to come into their bank account.

Payment in advance

A payment in advance is where a payment for goods or services is made ahead of schedule. This is not uncommon when dealing with larger orders as it helps the supplier to cover any 'out of pocket' expenses or to pay for the materials required to produce the order if they don't have enough capital to fund the purchase.

A payment in advance also helps safeguard the supplier against customers who don't pay or those that cancel a large order at the last minute.

Example – payment in advance

Where a supplier requests a 50% upfront payment from the buyer.

Payment on delivery

Payment on delivery is where the supplier will distribute goods to the customer and take payment for the goods upon delivery. If the customer does not pay for the goods, they are returned to the supplier.

Payment after invoice date

A payment after the invoice date gives the customer a certain number of calendar days to make payment 'after' the date of the invoice. The supplier can specify how many days this would be but quite commonly this is 10, 14, 30 or 60 days after the invoice date. This arrangement would be put in place as part of the supplier agreement.

Payment at the end of the month of invoice

A payment at the end of the month of invoice means that the supplier is expecting the money at the end of the month in which they have issued the invoice.

Example – payment at the end of month

Where an invoice is issued on the 15th September, the supplier will be expecting payment by the 30th September.

2.2 The Purchasing Process

The flow chart on the following page demonstrates the process that How Two Ltd would follow when making a purchase.

📖 **Case study**

How Two Ltd select a supplier

Some businesses will have an **approved supplier list**. This is a list of suppliers who are reliable and have the capacity to meet their customers needs. An approved supplier usually provides a consistent high level of service along with excellent quality standards of their products.

↓

They then raise a purchase order and send to the supplier

The purchase order in the purchasing process is exactly the same as that in the sales process. The only difference is that we are effectively the customer and therefore we are the ones completing the document and sending it to the supplier.

↓

How Two Ltd receive the goods or services from the supplier

↓

How Two Ltd check the delivery note against the goods received and sign the delivery note to say that they agree that it matches

The delivery note contains details as stated in the Sales section above. If there are any differences between the delivery note and the goods received, How Two Ltd. makes a note of any differences and queries them with the supplier. This would be noted before the delivery note was signed because otherwise How Two Ltd. could be invoiced for goods that they have never actually received.

↓

How Two Ltd complete a goods received note (GRN)

A **goods received note** is an internal document used to identify proof of goods actually received. See below for further explanation.

↓

How Two Ltd receive an invoice from the supplier in respect of the purchase

↓

How Two Ltd check the invoice received from the supplier against the purchase order, delivery note/goods received note to ensure that they have been invoice correctly

↓

Once satisfied that they have been invoiced accurately for their purchase, How Two Ltd make a payment to the supplier and record the expenditure.

2.3   The Goods Received Note (GRN)

A goods received note is an internal document that is used to document the receipt of goods or services. Upon delivery, the goods received will be checked against the delivery note sent from the supplier. If everything is present and correct, the customer will sign the delivery note to be returned to the supplier and will generate a GRN as proof of what has been received. This is then compared to the purchase order and the supplier invoice before payment is made.

📖 Case study

You work for How Two Ltd. and have been asked to prepare a goods received note using the following information:

Today is 31st October 20X7, there has been a delivery of goods into the warehouse. Yacob Solvez has checked the goods received and agrees that the details on the following delivery note are correct.

Using the information in the delivery note below, prepare the goods received note as requested, ensuring all of the relevant details are entered.

Delivery Note

To: **How Two Ltd.**
  1 Baker Street
  London
  WC1 8QT

From: **PC's R Us Ltd.**
  212 Wellington Street
  London
  WC12 8RD

Delivery Address:
1 Baker Street
London
WC1 8QT

Delivery note: 1056
Date of issue: 30th October 20X7
Purchase order number: PO5571

Delivery date: 31st October 20X7

Quantity	Code	DESCRIPTION
20	DKT476	Dall Laptop Model SKW665
25	ESMJA2	Epsan MJA2 projectors

Received by: ....

Signature: .... Date: ....

Goods Received Note

Goods Received Note		
Received From: PC's R Us 212 Wellington Street London WC12 8RD		
GRN number: 102		
Date goods received: 31st October 20X7		
Delivery note number: 1056		
Quantity	**Code**	**DESCRIPTION**
20	DKT476	Dall Laptop Model SKW665
25	ESMJA2	Epsan MJA2 projectors
Received by: YACOB SOLVEZ		
Signature: Y. Solvez .... Date: 31st October 20X7		

Note:

The details entered include the dates that the goods have been received, a goods received note number, the delivery note number from the supplier (so that it can be matched up later), the supplier details, quantities, descriptions and codes of the goods received and then details of the person who has received the goods into store.

✎ Test your understanding 6

Jessica has been asked to prepare a goods received note using the following information:

Today is 31st October 20X7, there has been a delivery of goods into the warehouse.

Jessica has checked the goods received and agree that the details on the following delivery note are correct.

The last GRN created was number 123.

Delivery Note:

Delivery Note		
Delivery note: 2212		
Date of issue: 30th October 20X7		
Purchase order number: PO5589		

To: How Two Ltd.
  1 Baker Street
  London
  WC1 8QT

From: Tablet World
  477 High Street
  Oxford
  OX10 5WD

Delivery Address:
1 Baker Street
London
WC1 8QT

Delivery date: 31st October 20X7

Quantity	Code	DESCRIPTION
15	SSX52	Samsong SX52 9" Tablet computers
15	DL656	Dall MC656 8" Tablet computers

Received by: ....

Signature: .... Date: ....

Goods Received Note:

Goods Received Note		
Received From:		

GRN number:
Date goods received:
Delivery note number:

Quantity	Code	DESCRIPTION

Received by: ....

Signature: .... Date:...

2.4 Statement of Account

At the end of each month, the supplier will summarise all the transactions that have taken place with the customer. This could include invoices, credit notes, and any payments received from the customer.

The statement of account will show the outstanding balance owing from the customer at the end of the month.

📖 **Case study**

Statement

How Two Ltd.

1 Baker Street
London
WC1 8QT
Tel: 020 7890 1234
Fax: 020 7890 1235

STATEMENT

To: IT Systems R Go
Date: 30th November 20X7

Date	Transaction	Debit £	Credit £	Balance £
1 November	Balance b/d	165.00		165.00
25 November	Invoice 5673	360.00		525.00
28 November	Credit Note 02452		72.00	453.00
30 November	Cash received		165.00	288.00

Notes

a) 1st November IT Systems R Go owed £165.00 from last month;

b) 25th November Invoice No 5673 for £360.00 has been added to the £165.00 to show a balance owing of £525.00;

c) 28th November Credit note No 02452 for £72.00 has been deducted from the £525.00 to show a balance at that date of £453.00;

d) 30th November IT Systems R Go have paid the amount owing at the beginning of the month, leaving a balance outstanding of £288.00.

2.5 Overview of the flow of transaction

The diagram below shows the typical flow of a transaction including the documents involved.

Dependent on whether it is a credit sale or a credit purchase, we will be looking at it from the perspective of the business or customer.

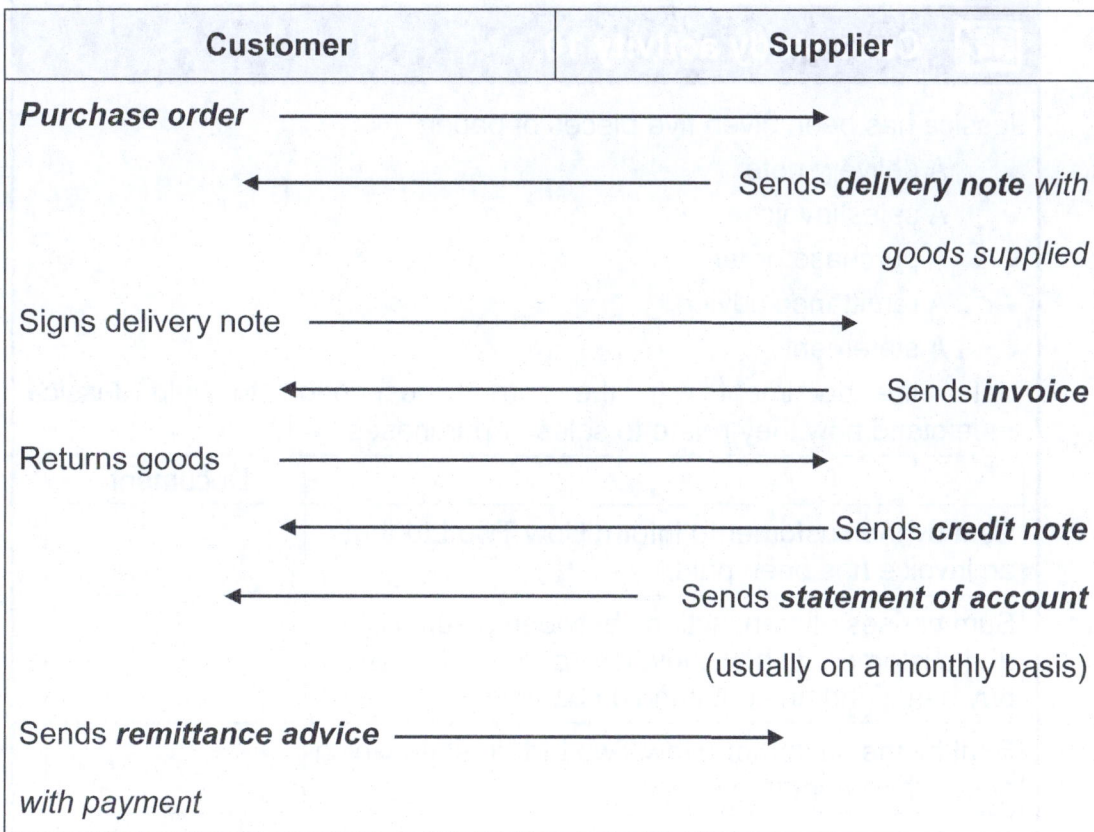

Customer	Supplier
Purchase order ⟶	
⟵	Sends *delivery note* with goods supplied
Signs delivery note ⟶	
⟵	Sends *invoice*
Returns goods ⟶	
⟵	Sends *credit note*
⟵	Sends *statement of account* (usually on a monthly basis)
Sends *remittance advice* ⟶ with payment	

3 Summary and further questions

In this chapter we have looked in detail at the documents used to record transactions for credit and cash customers. You should now know what information is required for each of these documents and you should be able to accurately generate them from given information.

Let us return to the case study to see how Jessica uses some of the documents to record sales and purchases at How Two Ltd.

📖 Case study activity 10

Jessica has been given five pieces of paper:
- A delivery note
- A sales invoice
- A purchase order
- A remittance advice
- A statement

Match the document with the correct description to help Jessica understand how they relate to sales or purchases.

	Document
Sent by the customer to inform How Two Ltd that an invoice has been paid.	
Summarises all transactions between a supplier and customer. It shows invoices and credit notes, payments and any outstanding balance.	
Sent by the customer (How Two Ltd) to state which goods they want to purchase	
Sent by the supplier to How Two Ltd with the goods when despatched	
Sent by the supplier to How Two Ltd to inform them of how much the goods cost	

📖 **Case study activity 11**

Jessica has been asked to prepare a delivery note using the information below:

Today is 29th October 20X7 and the following purchase order has been processed with the goods ready to be despatched to the customer. The last delivery note issued was number 1026 and the goods are due to be delivered tomorrow.

Using the information above along with the purchase order below, prepare the delivery note as requested, ensuring all of the relevant details are entered.

PURCHASE ORDER

Redshaw Cables
17 High Street
Manchester M1 6RS
Tel: 0161 741 2962
Fax: 0161 741 2963
Date: 23rd October 20X7
Purchase order no: P01562

To:	Delivery address
How Two Ltd.	(if different from above)
1 Baker Street	Four Lane Ends
London	New Mills
WC1 8QT	SK22 4LG

Product	Ref	Quantity	Price per unit (excl. VAT) £	Total (excl. VAT) £
HDMI Cables	HDMI62	20	15.00	300.00
Epsan SXA projectors	ESXA14	5	300.00	1,500.00

Signed: *J Johnson*
Purchasing Manager

Delivery Note:

Delivery Note	
To:	**From:**

Delivery Address:

Delivery note:
Date of issue:
Purchase order number:

Delivery date:

Quantity	Code	DESCRIPTION

Received by: ....

Signature: .... Date: ....

Case study activity 12

Jessica is looking at the account of one of How Two Ltd's biggest customers, NB Solutions Ltd, to see how much money is owed.

During the last month, NB Solutions have been sent two invoices by How Two Ltd for computer equipment that has been supplied. The two invoices total £457.98 and £69.65.

NB Solutions have also received a credit note for some mouse mats ordered in error and returned to How Two Ltd. This credit note was for a total of £58.60.

During the month, NB Solutions paid £200.00 to How Two Ltd.

a) What is the balance outstanding on NB Solutions' account?

b) What is the name of the document which will be sent to the customer to show these transactions and the balance outstanding?

Case study activity 13

Jessica has also been tasked with finding out how much money How Two Ltd need to pay one of their suppliers, MMC Direct.

At the start of the month, How Two Ltd owes MMC Direct £1,250.

The following transactions take place throughout the month:

Invoice for £1,100

Invoice for £3,250

Credit note for £500

Invoice for £2,225

Credit note for £225

a) What is the balance outstanding on How Two Ltd's credit account with MMC Direct?

b) What is the name of the document which Jessica should request is sent to How Two Ltd to show these transactions and the balance outstanding?

Case study activity 14

Jessica has checked that the balance is owing to MMC Direct Ltd is correct and needs to arrange payment. If How Two Ltd want to settle their account in full, what is the name of the document which will be sent to the supplier along with the payment, to show which transaction(s) it relates to?

Answers to chapter activities

📝 Test your understanding 1

Transaction	Document
A document sent by the supplier to the customer listing the goods or services supplied and requesting payment	Purchase Order
A document sent to a supplier detailing the goods that the customer wants to buy.	Invoice
A document sent to a customer to accompany the goods. The customer signs this upon receipt of their items.	Delivery Note

(Lines drawn: first transaction → Invoice; second transaction → Purchase Order; third transaction → Delivery Note)

📝 Test your understanding 2

	a) Credit Sale	b) Cash Sale
Net	£3,000	£2,800
VAT	£600	£560
Gross	£3,600	£3,360

Workings:

a) $3,600 \div 120 \times 100 = 3,000$

       $3,600 \div 120 \times 20 = 600$

b) $2,800 \div 100 \times 20 = 560$

       $2,800 \div 100 \times 120 = 3,360$

Test your understanding 3

Invoice 1 – The cost of the paper towels is £298.80.

Invoice 2 – £250.00 × 20/100 = £50.00. Therefore the VAT would be £50.

Invoice 3 – £480.00/1.2 = £400. £480 - £400 = £80.00. Therefore the VAT would be £80.

Test your understanding 4

INVOICE

Invoice to:
St Peter's Secondary School
141 St Petersgate
Manchester
M2 6KS

How Two Ltd
1 Baker Street
London
WC1 8QT

Tel: 0207 890 1234
Fax: 0207 890 1235

Deliver to:

As above

Invoice no: 95157
Tax point: 3rd November 17
VAT reg no: 618 2201 63
Delivery note no: 1114
Account no: SPS 1124

Code	Description	Quantity	VAT rate %	Unit price £	Amount net of VAT £
SMG 121	Samsong HD Monitor	5	20	69.99	349.95
SMG 123	Samsong HD Monitor	12	20	129.99	1,559.88
SMG 124	Samsong HD Monitor	8	20	149.99	1,199.92
					3,109.75
Bulk discount 15%					(466.46)
					2,643.29
VAT					528.65
Total amount payable					3,171.94

Test your understanding 5

Cavalier Beds
3 Brussels Road
County Road
Gloucester
GL6 6TH
Tel: 01456 698271   Fax: 01456 698272

Invoice to:		Invoice no:	67895
		Date:	28/10/X6
KP Furniture Ltd 9 Paris Street COLCHESTER CF25 1XY		VAT reg no:	488 7922 26
		Delivery note no:	6785
		Account no:	KP12

Code		Quantity	VAT rate	Unit price £	Amount excl of VAT £
MAT15K	Deluxe Mattress	5	20%	98.00	490.00
Trade discount 10%					49.00
Subtotal					441.00
VAT					88.20
Total amount payable					529.20

Test your understanding 6

Goods Received Note

Goods Received Note		
GRN number: 124		
Date goods received: 31st October 20X7		
Delivery note number: 2212		
Received From:		
Tablet World		
477 High Street		
Oxford		
OX10 5WD		
Quantity	**Code**	**DESCRIPTION**
15	SSX52	**Samsung SX52 9" Tablet computers**
15	DL656	**Dall MC656 8" Tablet computers**
Received by: *JESSICA HOWARD*		
Signature: *J. Howard* .... Date: *31ˢᵗ October 20X7*		

Case study activity 10

	Document
Sent by the customer to inform How Two Ltd that an invoice has been paid.	**A remittance advice**
Summarises all transactions between a supplier and customer. It shows invoices and credit notes, payments and any outstanding balance.	**A statement**
Sent by the customer (How Two Ltd) to state which goods they want to purchase	**A purchase order**
Sent by the supplier to How Two Ltd with the goods when despatched	**A delivery note**
Sent by the supplier to How Two Ltd to inform them of how much the goods cost	**A sales invoice**

Case study activity 11

Delivery Note

To: Redshaw Cables
17 High Street
Manchester
M1 6RS

From: How Two Ltd.
1 Baker Street
London
WC1 8QT

Delivery Address:
Four Lane Ends
New Mills
SK22 4LG

Delivery note: 1027
Date of issue: 29th October 20X7
Purchase order number: PO1562

Delivery date: 30th October 20X7

Quantity	Code	DESCRIPTION
20	HDMI62	HDMI Cables
5	ESXA14	Epsan SXA projectors

Received by: ....

Signature: ....   Date: ....

Case study activity 12

a) What is the balance outstanding on NB Solutions' account?

£269.03

b) What is the name of the document which will be sent to the customer to show these transactions and the balance outstanding?

Statement of Account

Case study activity 13

a) What is the balance outstanding on How Two Ltd's credit account with MMC Direct?

£7,100

b) What is the name of the document which Jessica should request is sent to How Two Ltd to show these transactions and the balance outstanding?

Statement of Account

Case study activity 14

A remittance advice is the document to be sent with the payment.

Checking documentation

4

Introduction

In the previous chapter we looked at the different types of business documentation used by a bookkeeper and the purposes for each. Here, we will look at the importance of ensuring that these documents are accurate. We will compare documents in the purchasing process to ensure that they are accurate.

We will also look at the different types of errors that could occur and what action should be taken should this happen.

KNOWLEDGE	CONTENTS
Understand the role of a bookkeeper 1.3 Importance of working with accuracy **Process customer and supplier transactions** 3.2 Check purchase invoices and credit notes	1 Business procedures 2 Checking documents 3 Summary and further questions

1 Business procedures

1.1 Case study: an introduction

📖 Case study

Jessica is now feeling very confident about her bookkeeping skills and has been working on processing sales and purchasing documentation for a few days now. She feels as though she is really starting to understand the systems and processes around this.

Jessica is keen to continue looking at How Two Ltd's finances and helping to balance the books. Her manager makes Jessica aware of the impact it could have on the organisation if these documents are not accurate and the consequences as a result of them being incorrect.

Therefore it is vital that Jessica understands the importance of checking all business documentation before processing it. As a result, Jessica is now going to explore in more detail how to check business documents for accuracy and what to do if she discovers discrepancies or errors.

1.2 The need to follow business procedures

It is essential to follow business procedures when dealing with sales and purchases. This will ensure that the processes are completed fully and accurately as required by the organisation. Failure to do so could result in deadlines being missed, which ultimately causes issues for the business.

For example, if goods are not checked properly upon receipt this could lead to the company creating a goods received note for incorrect items of stock and they could be charged incorrectly for items that they have never received.

If there are many queries raised in relation to goods received, this could lead to further complications when it comes to the payment run, and could result in the internal deadline being missed. If this was the case, the supplier may not receive their payment on time which could damage the business relationship with the supplier.

It is important to follow the correct procedures for the following reasons:

- It helps to avoid errors – if the process of completing business documents is followed properly, the number of errors made will be minimal. If errors are made in paying suppliers, i.e. the business

overpays them or makes duplicate payments to the supplier, this could lead to cash flow problems for the business. As a result, the business may find that they don't have enough money to pay their suppliers and could therefore have to source money from elsewhere (e.g. a loan or overdraft). This is an expensive option for the business and could have a negative effect on the overall profit or loss.

- It helps to avoid missing internal or external deadlines – this is key to the smooth operation of the sales and purchasing departments. If deadlines are missed, a backlog of work will be created. If you get behind with your work, you could rush to try to get back on top of it which creates a risk of errors being made.

- It ensures processes are completed as required by the business – every business has different needs and requirements from business documents. Invoices, credit notes, purchase orders, delivery notes, goods returned notes and goods received notes will look different depending on the company that has created them. The basic information within these documents however, will remain the same.

- It maintains good business relationships with customers and suppliers – if procedures are followed accurately then the number of errors or queries will be minimal, payments will be made on time and therefore business relationships will remain positive. For example, if a supplier is underpaid, this could lead to them refusing to process any further orders of inventory. If this was the case, there could be delays with fulfilling customer orders therefore this would have a negative impact on both the customer and supplier relationship.

1.3 Ensuring procedures are followed correctly

Following procedures correctly is of paramount importance to the smooth operation of an organisation.

The following steps give you an idea of how to ensure that you are performing work-related tasks correctly to prevent wasting time tracing and correcting errors.

- Ensure that business documentation is completed fully and accurately – make sure that all quantities, prices and discounts are cross checked for accuracy and that all item codes, customer or supplier codes and document reference number e.g. PO numbers or delivery note numbers are correct too.

- Complete all documents on time – within the sales and purchasing departments there will be deadlines that need to be met. It is highly likely that someone else within the department is relying on the completion of your work before they can complete theirs. Failure to meet deadlines will cause delays in sales invoices being sent out to the customer and therefore will delay the payment coming in from the customer. It could also create delays in payments to suppliers which could cause issues in terms of receiving stock to fulfil customer orders. This will have a negative effect of business relationships with both customers and suppliers.

- Ensure that the correct authorisation has been obtained – not having the correct authorisation before sending out documents or processing documentation can lead to errors being made within the system. Obtaining authorisation means that your work has been checked and it has been agreed with someone more senior who has the ability to make business decisions. Failure to do so could lead to incorrect information being entered into the accounts.

An overstatement or understatement of figures within the accounting records could lead to incorrect profit or loss figures being recorded. It is imperative that this is accurate for accurate business decisions to be made. For example, if a profit figure is overstated, the director could start thinking about expansion plans for the business. If the business doesn't have the correct resource to be able to put this into place then this could lead the business to fail.

✎ Test your understanding 1

Which ONE of the following is a likely outcome of procedures NOT being followed correctly?

	✓
Deadlines being met	
Greater customer satisfaction	
Increased profits	
Errors when completing documentation and/or payments	

---

2 Checking documents

2.1 Dealing with common errors and discrepancies

If there are errors when checking purchasing documentation, it depends on what the error is as to how it should be dealt with.

There are many different errors or discrepancies that may be found when checking documents but the main ones that you will come across on an invoice might include:

- calculation errors

- incorrect VAT calculations
- incorrect type/quantity of goods
- incorrect prices being charged for the goods.

If this is the case then the invoice should be rejected and a dispute raised with the supplier.

Another common example of discrepancies involves the goods themselves. If the goods are damaged or the incorrect goods have been delivered then the buyer will return the goods to the supplier with a goods returned note, requesting a credit note to be issued from the supplier. Upon receipt of the credit note, the buyer would need to check the goods returned note against the credit note to make sure that there are no discrepancies.

The following information should be checked:

- Do the purchase order numbers match?
- Do the details of the goods returned match, including, the quantity, price and description?
- Have the same % of discounts been applied to the credit note?
- Has the VAT been calculated correctly?

If an error or discrepancy is discovered on a credit note or goods returned note, the issue should be raised and the credit note should not be recorded or processed in the accounts.

Test your understanding 2

Which of the following should be checked on documentation relating to sales and purchases to identify potential errors? (Tick ALL correct answers).

	✓
Purchase Order number	
Quantity of goods supplied	
Prices of goods supplied	
VAT calculation on goods supplied	
Registered charity no of supplier	
Company logo of supplier	
Discount given by supplier	

2.2   Case study: an example of checking documents

📖 **Case study**

Jessica has been asked to check the following documentation to see whether there are any discrepancies.

PURCHASE ORDER

How Two Ltd.
1 Baker Street
London
WC1 8QT
Tel: 0207 3972 226

Date: 25th October 20X7
Purchase order no: P01671

To: MMC Direct 12 Saunders Street London, WC4 VCV Tel: 0207 3972 226	Delivery address (if different from above) **As above**

Product	Ref	Quantity	Price per unit (excl. VAT) £	Total (excl. VAT) £
Koduk SNS200 Printer	SNS200	10	99.99	999.99
Koduk SNS400 Printer	SNS400	15	149.99	2,249.85
Epsan EPS500 Printer	EPS500	20	109.00	2,810.00
Signed:	*A Khan* Purchasing Manager			

Delivery Note:

Delivery Note	
To: How Two Ltd. 1 Baker Street London WC1 8QT	**From:** MMC Direct 12 Saunders Street London WC4 VCV

Delivery note: 2331   **Date of issue:** 30th October 20X7
Purchase order number: PO1671

Delivery Address:
12 Saunders Street
London
WC4 VCV

Delivery date: 31st October 20X7

Quantity	Code	DESCRIPTION
15	SNS201	Koduk SNS201 Printer
10	SNS400	Koduk SNS400 Printer
15	EPS500	Epsan EPS500 Printer

Received by: ....

Signature: .... Date: ....

Goods Received Note:

Good Received Note
Received From: MMC Direct   12 Saunders Street   London   WC4 VCV

Delivery note number: 2333
Purchase order number: PO1671

Quantity	Code	DESCRIPTION
15	SNS200	Koduk SNS200 Printer
10	SNS400	Koduk SNS400 Printer
15	EPS500	Epsan EPS500 Printer

Received by: *YACOB SOLVEZ*...

Signature: *Y. Solvez*.............. Date: *31st October 20X7*..........

When checking the documents for accuracy the following errors have been identified:

- When checking the calculations of prices on the PO the total price for the Epsan EPS500 Printer is incorrect. The order states 20 @ £109.00 which equals £2,180.00. The total price on the order has been entered as £2,810. This has been signed by A Khan (Purchasing Manager) to say that it is correct.

- The incorrect quantities have been delivered.

  The PO states:

  - 10 x Koduk SNS200 Printers
  - 15 x Koduk SNS400 Printers
  - 20 x Epsan EPS500 Printers

  The delivery note states:

  - 15 x Koduk SNS201 Printers
  - 10 x Koduk SNS400 Printers
  - 15 x Epsan EPS500 Printers

- Some incorrect items have also been delivered. How Two Ltd. ordered 10 x Koduk SNS200 Printers but 15 x Koduk SNS201 Printers have been delivered.

- The supplier address has been entered as the delivery address on the delivery note. This should be the address of How Two Ltd.

- Yacob Solvez has completed a GRN even though the items delivered do not match the PO.

- Yacob has entered the delivery note number incorrectly on the GRN which will cause issues when dealing with the queries.

- On the GRN Yacob states that 15 x Koduk SNS200 Printers have been received when in actual fact it was 15 x Koduk SNS201 Printers. This is the wrong item and therefore should not be accepted. If he has signed to say that the correct item has been received this could cause issues when raising a query with the supplier.

As all of the above is incorrect, this should be referred back to the Purchasing Manager to resolve.

3 Summary and further questions

In this chapter we have looked at how invoices and credit notes should be checked in business. You should now be able to check the relevant purchasing documentation for errors and you should understand why this is important. You should know what to do if you discover any discrepancies within a place of work and how these should be dealt with.

We will return to the How Two Ltd case study to further practice checking documentation.

📖 Case study activity 15

Jessica has been asked to review the following price list and check whether the Purchase Order has been completed correctly.

She has then been asked to check the additional documentation to see whether there are any discrepancies between the PO, delivery note and GRN.

Price List		
Item description	**Item Code**	**Price (excluding VAT)**
HT Notebook	HT477	345.00
Dall Notepad	DL90X	350.00
Tashibo Note Perfect	TNP450	295.00
Micrasaft Touch Pro	MTP225	399.00

PURCHASE ORDER

How Two Ltd.

1 Baker Street

London

WC1 8QT

Tel: 0207 890 1234

Date: 29th October 20X7
Purchase order no: P01682

To: Tech Unlimited 427 Lever Street Manchester, M1 2LF Tel: 0161 484 7711	Delivery address (if different from above) **As above**

Product	Ref	Quantity	Price per unit (excl. VAT) £	Total (excl. VAT) £
HT Notebook	HT477	5	354.00	1,770.00
Micrasaft Touch Pro	MTP225	7	399.00	2,793.00
Dall Notepad	DL90X	8	350.00	2,400.00
Signed: *A Khan* Purchasing Manager				

Delivery Note:

Delivery Note	
To: How Two Ltd. 1 Baker Street London WC1 8QT	**From:** Tech Unlimited 427 Lever Street Manchester M1 2LF
Delivery note: 2401 **Purchase order number:** PO1682	**Date of issue:** 31st Oct 20X7

Delivery Address:
1 Baker Street
London
WC1 8QT

Delivery date: 1st November 20X7

Quantity	Code	DESCRIPTION
5	HT478	HT Notebook
8	MTP225	Micrasaft Touch Pro
7	DL90X	Dall Notepad

Received by: ....

Signature: .... Date: ....

Goods Received Note:

Good Received Note		
Received From: MMC Direct 12 Saunders Street London WC4 VCV		
Delivery note number: 2401 **Purchase order number:** PO1682		

Quantity	Code	DESCRIPTION
5	HT477	HT Notebook
7	MTP225	Micrasaft Touch Pro
8	DL90X	Dall Notepad

Received by: *YACOB SOLVEZ*...

Signature: *Y. Solvez*................. Date: *31st October 2017*..........

Case study activity 16

Jessica has been asked to review the following goods returned note and check whether the credit note has been completed correctly.

Good Returned Note

MMC Direct	To: How Two Ltd.
12 Saunders Street	1 Baker Street
London	London
WC4 VCV	WC1 8QT
VAT Number: 231 7787 543	

Goods returned note number: 1023
Purchase order number: PO193

Date: 31st October 2017

Quantity	Code	DESCRIPTION	£
1	HT477	HT Notebook	225.00
2	MTP225	Micrasaft Touch Pro	500.00
1	DL90X	Dall Notepad	200.00

Received by: *YACOB SOLVEZ* ....

Signature: *Y. Solvez*............... Date: *31st October 2017* ....

Credit Note

How Two Ltd.	MMC Direct
1 Baker Street	12 Saunders Street
London	London
WC1 8QT	WC4 VCV

Date: 5th November 2017
Credit note number: CN440
Purchase order number: PO182

Quantity	Code	DESCRIPTION	£
1	HP499	HP Notebook	225.00
1	MTP225	Micrasaft Touch Pro	500.00
1	DL90X	Dall Notepad	200.00
		Net	925.00
		VAT	155.00
		Total	1,080.00

Answers to chapter activities

Test your understanding 1

	✓
Deadlines being met	
Greater customer satisfaction	
Increased profits	
Errors when completing documentation and/or payments	✓

Test your understanding 2

	✓
Purchase Order number	✓
Quantity of goods supplied	✓
Prices of goods supplied	✓
VAT calculation on goods supplied	✓
Registered charity no of supplier	
Company logo of supplier	
Discount given by supplier	✓

Case study activity 15

The following errors and discrepancies can be identified:

- The HT Notebook has been priced at £354 on the purchase order instead of £345.

- The total of the HT Notebooks should be £1,725 if the correct price of £345 had been stated however £1,770 has been entered on the PO.

- The total of the Dall notepads should be £2,800 but £2,400 has been entered on the PO.

- The incorrect product code has been entered on the delivery note for the HT Notebook.

- The incorrect quantities have been entered on the delivery note for the Micrasaft Touch Pro and the Dall Notepad, 7 Micrasaft Touch Pros had been ordered but the delivery note states 8 have been delivered and 8 Dall Notepads had been ordered but the delivery note states that 7 have been delivered.

- The goods received note matches the purchase order but due to the discrepancies on the delivery note this does not match the goods received note.

Case study activity 16

The following errors and discrepancies can be identified:

- The incorrect purchase order number has been stated on the credit note

- The incorrect product code has been stated on the credit note for the HP Notebook, this should be HT477 not HP499

- The goods returned note states that 2 Micrasaft Touch Pros have been returned but only one has been credited

- 2 Micrasaft Touch Pros have been returned which in total come to £500. Only 1 has been entered on the credit note but the price state is still £500

- The VAT has been calculated on the credit note. It should be £185 not £155.

- The total of the credit note is incorrect, this should be £1,110 not £1,080.

Books of prime entry

5

Introduction

In the previous chapter you looked at the documents that are used in cash and credit transactions. These documents now need to be summarised in **books of prime entry**.

As the documents are recorded regularly, these books are also known as **day books.**

KNOWLEDGE	CONTENTS
Understand the role of a bookkeeper 1.3 Importance of working with accuracy **Process customer and supplier transactions** 3.3 Record sales and purchase invoices and credit notes in the books of prime entry 3.4 Identify outstanding amounts for individual customers and suppliers **Process receipts and payments** 4.1 Enter receipts and payments into a cash book 4.2 Use the cash book to calculate closing amounts of cash in hand and cash in the bank	1 Documents used to record transactions with customers 2 Documents used to record transactions with suppliers 3 Receipts and payments 4 The cash book 5 The petty cash book 6 Batch control 7 Summary and further questions

1 Documents used to record transactions with customers

1.1 Introduction: case study and overview

📖 Case study

Having looked at the documents used in cash and credit transactions, Jessica has gained a greater awareness of how important accuracy is when dealing with business documentation and also the need to check them carefully to ensure that there are no errors.

Extremely happy with Jessica's progress, her manager now feels that she is competent to accomplish bookkeeping tasks and is ready to move on to the next stage. To do so, Jessica now needs to learn how to summarise the documents she has encountered into the books of prime entry, also known as day books.

Her manager provides her with an overview of the different day books she needs to learn to use to record transactions with customers (below).

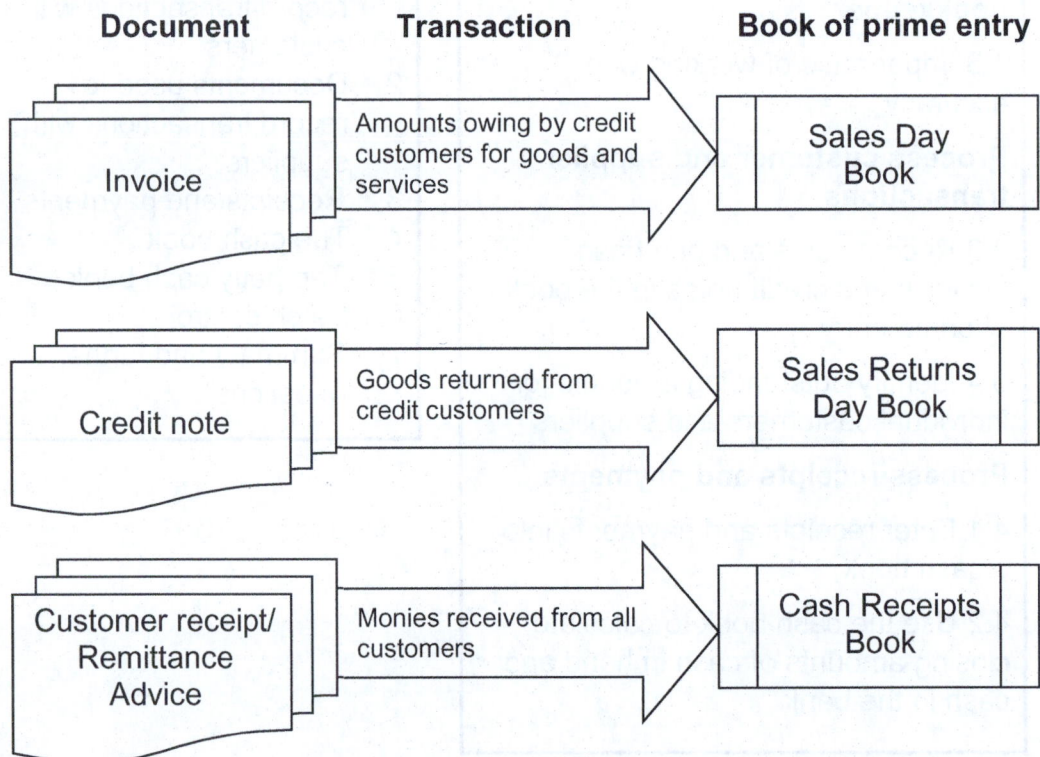

Document	Transaction	Book of prime entry
Invoice	Amounts owing by credit customers for goods and services	Sales Day Book
Credit note	Goods returned from credit customers	Sales Returns Day Book
Customer receipt/ Remittance Advice	Monies received from all customers	Cash Receipts Book

1.2   The sales day book (SDB)

The sales day book records individual invoices issued to credit customers within one day, week or month. It is basically a list which is totalled at the end of the specified period to indicate how much a company has made in sales, how much VAT they owe to HMRC in respect of those sales and how much they are owed in total by their customers. It will then be used to perform double entry bookkeeping, which you will learn about in the AAT Foundation Certificate.

Example

SALES DAY BOOK

Date	Customer	Reference	Invoice number	Total £	VAT £	Sales £
1 July	Althams Ltd	ALT01	45787	120.00	20.00	100.00
2 July	Broadhurst plc	BRO02	45788	240.00	40.00	200.00
			TOTALS	360.00	60.00	300.00

Notes

- The reference number is the code number of the customer's account in the sales ledger this information can be found on the invoice.
- The invoice number is the number of the invoice issued for each sale.
- The Sales column is the total value of the goods sold as shown on the invoice after deducting trade discount, i.e. net of VAT.
- The amount of VAT is recorded in a separate column to show the amount owing to HMRC for these invoices.
- The Total column shows the total amount due from credit customers (Receivables).

Example

Farley's AV Supplies sell a variety of audio visual products for both business customers and online for the general public.

On 3rd January, they have recorded two trade sales to customers on account.

Invoice number 365 to JBU Wines is made up as follows:

	£
Sale of 20 AV lead packs at £5 per unit	100.00
Less: 20% trade discount	(20.00)
	80.00
VAT (£80 × 20%)	16.00
Total invoice value	96.00

Invoice number 366 to Stop-it Holidays is made up as follows:

	£
Sale of 5 headphone & charger sets at £30 per unit	150.00
Less: 10% trade discount	(15.00)
	135.00
VAT (£135.00 × 20%)	27.00
Total invoice value	162.00

Farley AV Supplies' sales day book would therefore look like this:

Date	Customer	Reference	Invoice number	Total £	VAT £	Sales £
3/1	JBU Wines	JBU1708	365	96.00	16.00	80.00
3/1	Stop-it Holidays	STO1999	366	162.00	27.00	135.00
			TOTALS	**258.00**	**43.00**	**215.00**

1.3 The sales returns day book

Credit notes, also known as sales returns, are usually entered in a 'sales returns day book'.

This is similar to the sales day book, and the columns are used in the same way. The only difference is that instead of having a column for the invoice number, there is a column for the 'credit note number'. This is because when the goods are returned by customers a credit note is issued.

Example

Farley's AV Supplies receive two returns from customers in the first week of May.

Credit note number 072 for Pilgrim Sports and Leisure on 1st May is made up as follows:

	£
Return of 2 faulty television stands at £55 each	110.00
VAT (£110 × 20%)	22.00
Total credit note value	132.00

Credit note number 073 for Crabtree's Circus on 3rd May is made up as follows:

	£
Return of 4 large venue speakers at £195 each	780.00
VAT (£780 × 20%)	156.00
Total credit note value	936.00

Farley AV Supplies' sales returns day book would therefore look like this:

SALES RETURNS DAY BOOK

Date	Customer	Reference	Credit note number	Total £	VAT £	Sales returns £
1/5	Pilgrim Sports and Leisure	PSLR04	072	110.00	22.00	132.00
3/5	Crabtree's Circus	CCR05	073	780.00	156.00	936.00
			TOTALS	890.00	178.00	1,068.00

In some businesses the level of sales returns are fairly low and therefore it is not justified to keep a separate sales returns day book. In these cases any credit notes that are issued for sales returns are recorded as negative amounts in the sales day book.

For the purpose of this assessment, a sales returns day book will be used to record credit note transactions.

2 Documents used to record transactions with suppliers

2.1 Introduction: case study and overview

📖 Case study

As Jessica has understood the different day books used for customer transactions, her manager now provides an overview of those to record transactions with suppliers (below).

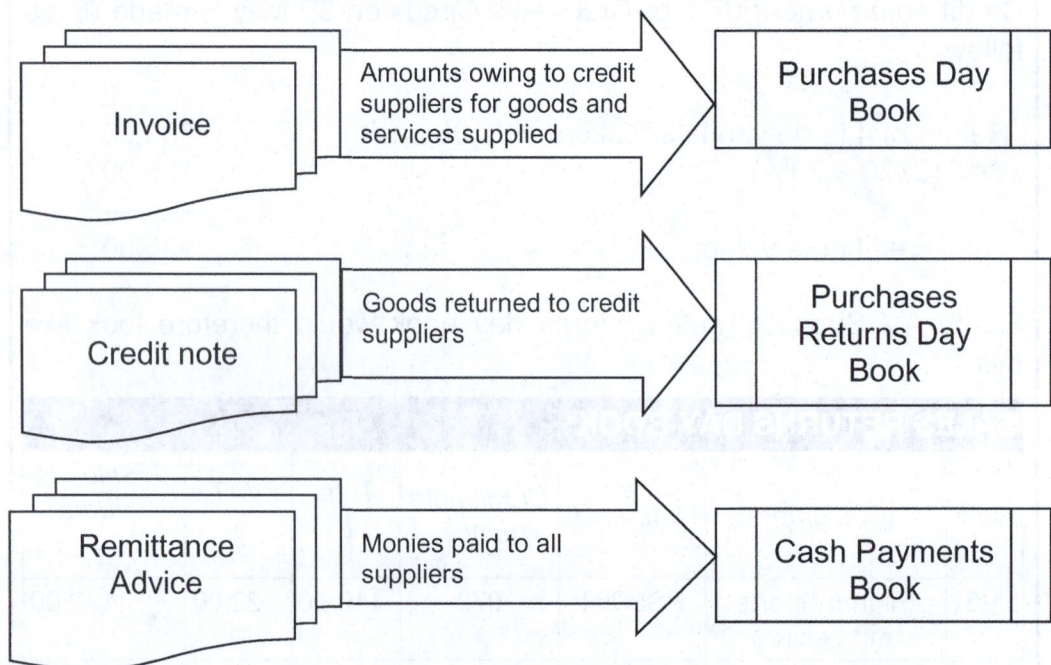

Invoice	Amounts owing to credit suppliers for goods and services supplied	Purchases Day Book
Credit note	Goods returned to credit suppliers	Purchases Returns Day Book
Remittance Advice	Monies paid to all suppliers	Cash Payments Book

2.2   The purchases day book

As seen earlier in the chapter, credit sales are recorded in the 'sales day book'. In the case of credit purchases, we have the 'purchases day book'.

The purchases day book is simply a list of the purchases invoices that are to be processed for a given period (e.g. a week).

In its simplest form, the purchases day book will comprise just the names of the suppliers and the amount of the invoices received in the week.

Example

PURCHASES DAY BOOK

Date	Supplier	Reference	Invoice number	Total £	VAT £	Purchases £
1 Sept 17	W E L Ltd	Q73243	56712	1,800	300	1,500
3 Sept 17	Vivalitee plc	L73244	AV942	402	67	335
			TOTALS	2,202	367	1,835

Purchases returns are entered in a 'purchases returns day book'. This looks similar to the purchases day book, and the columns are used in the same way. The only difference is that instead of having a column for the invoice number, there is a column for the 'credit note number'. This is because when the goods are sent back the business will receive a credit note from the supplier.

Example

PURCHASES RETURNS DAY BOOK

Date	Supplier	Reference	Credit note number	Total £	VAT £	Purchases returns £
1 Sept 17	Lazza & Co	RET732	AR678	300	60	360
4 Sept 17	BFBC	RET733	09132	185	37	222
			TOTALS	485	97	582

In some businesses the level of purchases returns are fairly low and therefore it is not necessary to keep a separate purchases returns day book.

In these cases any credit notes that are received for purchases returns are recorded as negative amounts in the purchases day book.

Example

You work in the accounts department of R Porte Manufacturing Ltd and one of your tasks is to sort the documents before they are entered in to the correct books of prime entry.

From the following documents, identify which book of prime entry it should be recorded in.

Document 1

R Moore Fashions

12 Dutch Corner
High Wycombe
HG4 7NQ

Invoice no: 005673
Tax point: 14 July 2018

INVOICE

To: R Porte Manufacturing Ltd
   5 Ventoux Crescent, Cardiff, CA2 3HU

Product	Quantity	Price per unit £	Total £
Cargo pants	5	25.00	125.00
T-shirts	10	15.00	150.00
			275.00
		VAT 20%	55.00
		Total	330.00
Payment terms: 30 days net			

Answer: You are dealing with documents for R Porte Manufacturing.

This invoice is sent **to** you at R Porte Manufacturing, so you have received it from R Moore Fashions, who must be the supplier.

Therefore, this is a supplier invoice and should be entered into the **purchases day book.**

The entry would appear as follows:

Date	Supplier	Reference	Invoice number	Total £	VAT £	Purchases £
14 July 18	R Moore Fashions	MORS78	005673	330	55	275
			TOTALS	330	55	275

Document 2

R Porte Manufacturing Ltd

5 Ventoux Crescent
Cardiff
CA2 3HU

Credit Note no: 05876
Tax point: 16 July 2018

CREDIT NOTE

To: Birnies Biscuits
 Elysee Avenue, Mitcham, MA3 6ZT

Product	Quantity	Price per unit (£)	Total (£)
Packing cases	4	5.00	20.00
		VAT 20%	4.00
		Total	24.00
Payment terms: 30 days net			

Answer: Remember, you are dealing with documents for R Porte Manufacturing.

This credit note is sent **to** Birnies Biscuits, so they must be the customer.

Therefore, this is a customer credit note and should be entered into the **sales returns day book.**

The entry would appear as follows:

Date	Customer	Reference	Credit note no	Total £	VAT £	Sales return £
16 July 18	Birnies Biscuits	BIR732	05876	24.00	4.00	20.00
			TOTALS	**24.00**	**4.00**	**20.00**

3 Receipts and payments

3.1 Cash receipts and payments

There are many different ways a business can make and receive payments. A lot of businesses make electronic payments; however, many customers still pay in cash or by writing a cheque. When physical payments are received by an organisation, the monies will need to be paid into the business's bank account.

In a cash sale or purchase, the transaction is much simpler. The customer will probably place an order verbally and payment is always made as soon as the customer receives the goods or services. Payment for cash sales or purchases are usually made by cash, credit or debit card.

The customer will need a copy of the sales receipt in case they need to return them to the supplier.

🔍 Definition

Monies – A term used to describe all types of payments and receipts including cash, cheques and direct bank transfers.

3.2 Paying-in slips

All business organisations are provided with a paying-in book by the bank. Each paying-in book contains paying-in slips. When money is received from customers in cash or by cheque, it is paid into the bank and is accompanied by one of the completed paying-in slips.

If your job is to pay money into the bank, you will need to complete and sign the bank paying-in slip taken from the paying-in book. The paying-in slip is then given to the bank cashier who will check it against the monies being paid in to the bank.

3.3 Example of a paying-in slip

Today's date

Cash and Cheques sums

Paying-in slip	To be used to pay into a HSBC Bank or first direct account only	£50 Notes
Date		£20 Notes 80 - 00
Cashier's Stamp	Bank	£10 Notes 110 - 00
	HSBC Bank plc/first direct *Delete as appropriate*	£5 Notes 10 - 00
	Account Holding Branch	£ & 1 Notes
		£2 Coin 22 - 00
	Customer's Name	£1 Coin 3 - 00
	Account holder's name	50p
	Name and address of person paying in (if not the customer)	20p
		Silver
		Bronze
	Sorting Code Number Account Number	Total Total Cash 25 - 00
Number of cheques	4 0	Cheques Total Cheques 30 - 00
		£ 255 - 00

Please do not write or mark below this line or fold this voucher

⑉000000   70

Number of cheques   **Sort Code**   **Account Number**   **Grand Total**
(Written clearly like this example)

(Source: www.hsbc.co.uk)

3.4 Paying-in requirements and records

You only need to enter the number of cheques being paid in and the total amount on the front of the paying in slip. On the back of the paying in slip you should write a list of the cheques being paid in.

The paying-in stub is the part of the paying-in slip which stays in the paying-in book and is a record for the organisation of the amounts paid into the bank. Sometimes a business may keep a separate list of monies received so that they can cross reference it the bank statement to ensure the correct amount has been paid in, or with the paying in slip should issues arise further on down the line.

Test your understanding 1

Today's date is 19 November 2017.

Jessica has been asked to complete a bank paying-in slip for the money received today, which is as follows:

Notes	Coins	Cheques
3 x £20 notes	25 x £1 coins	Thomas £1,500.00
15 x £10 notes	8 x 50p coins	Friebe £ 750.00
20 x £5 notes	20 x 10p coins	

Complete the paying-in slip below:

Date:	ABC Bank plc Manchester	£50 notes	
		£20 notes	
		£10 notes	
	Account How Two Ltd	£5 notes	
		£2 coin	
		£1 coin	
No of cheques	Paid in by *Jessica Howard*	Other coin	
		Total cash	
	Sort Code Account No	Cheques	
	25-22-78 30087251	Total £	

Test your understanding 2

When Jessica asked her manager to check over the paying in slip to ensure that she had completed it correctly before taking it to the bank, she was asked why it is important that the paying-in slip is signed and dated.

What would Jessica's response have been?

3.5   The use of cheques

When a person (or organisation) writes a cheque they are instructing their bank to transfer a specified amount of money from their bank account to the bank account of the recipient of the cheque – the payee.

If the cheque hasn't been completed correctly the bank may return it to the payee. The payee will then have to ask for a replacement cheque from the organisation.

As this causes delays in the payment process, it is important that the cheque is completed correctly in the first place.

3.6   Cheque requirements

For a cheque to be valid it should include:

- **Payee name**   The payee is the person or organisation to whom the cheque is written. The payee's name should exactly match the name on their bank account.

- **Date**   The date that the cheque is written must include the day, month and the year. A cheque that is more than 6 months old is invalid and the bank will not accept the cheque.

- **Words** The pounds part of the amount being paid must be written in words but the pence part can be written in numbers. If the amount is a whole number of pounds then you should write 'ONLY' after the amount to prevent someone changing the figure.

- **Numbers** The amount being paid should be written in numbers in the box on the right hand side of the cheque. The amount in numbers should exactly match the amount written in words.

- **Signature** The cheque should be signed by an authorised signatory of the organisation.

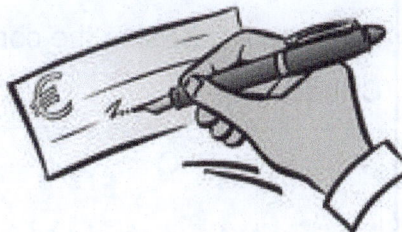

🔍 Definition

Signatories – a person or persons who are authorised to sign cheques on behalf of an organisation.

💡 Example

ABC Bank PLC	Date: 30th January 20X7
Payee: *Mr John Smith*	
	£350.00
Three hundred and fifty pounds only	MISS ANNE JONES

CHEQUE NO	SORT CODE	ACCOUNT NO
00017	32-32-68	5552222

✏ Test your understanding 3

Today's date is 29th November 2017 and Jessica has been given the following cheques to complete.

Fill in the gaps using the correct numbers, words and/or date.

Cheque A

ABC Bank PLC	Date: 29th November, 2017
Payee: *NB Solutions Ltd*	
Five hundred pounds ONLY	on behalf of How Two Ltd
	J Howard

CHEQUE NO	SORT CODE	ACCOUNT NO
04312	25-22-78	30087251

Cheque B

ABC Bank PLC	Date: 29th November, 2017
Payee: *Armistead & Co*	
	250.50
	on behalf of How Two Ltd
	J Howard

CHEQUE NO	SORT CODE	ACCOUNT NO
04313	25-22-78	30087251

Cheque C

ABC Bank PLC	Date:
Payee: *Mr P Sagan*	
	25.20
Twenty five pounds and 20p only	on behalf of How Two Ltd
	J Howard

CHEQUE NO	SORT CODE	ACCOUNT NO
04314	25-22-78	30087251

> **📝 Test your understanding 4**
>
> Cheques can be signed by anyone in an organisation. True or False?

3.7   Direct debits and standing orders

A **direct debit** is an electronic payment set up by you. You instruct your bank or building society to allow a third party to take money from your bank account at a specified time.

The amounts paid could vary in amount but you will have been informed of how much this will be and when the money will be taken, by the company you are making payment to.

An example of this might be when you are paying your gas or electric bill. The total of the bill will vary from month on month depending on how much gas and electric you use; however, you will have been sent the bill in advance of the money being taken from your bank and this will advise you of the date on which the money will be taken.

A **standing order** is where you set up a regular automated payment to be taken from your bank at a specified time in the month e.g. the 1st of every month. With a standing order, the amounts to be paid are fixed for a certain amount of time. An example of this might be when you are paying your rent. Payments of rent will be the same amount to be paid at the same time each month, in this case, a standing order would be the most suitable method of payment. Standing orders can be amended or cancelled at any time.

Usually, a business will have a direct debit or standing order schedule set up which is basically list of payments that they are expecting to go out of their bank account. This helps them to cross reference payments on their bank statement to ensure the correct ones have been made.

3.8   BACS and faster payments

A **BACS** payment is an automated system that is used to make payment from one bank to another. They are mainly used for direct debits so once you have given permission for an organisation to take payment from your bank account, they will usually do this via the BACS system. A BACS payment takes 3 days to clear in a bank account so if payment was made on Monday, it wouldn't appear in the recipient's bank until Wednesday.

KAPLAN PUBLISHING

113

A **faster payment** is an electronic payment that can be made online via internet banking or over the phone. A faster payment is usually made within two hours of making the payment meaning that the money will clear in the recipient's bank account the same day. Both banks have to be part of the faster payments service for this method of payment to be an option however nowadays this is a common service used by businesses to make quick payments to suppliers of goods or services.

Test your understanding 5

Match the definitions with the correct words used in banking

A person who is authorised to sign documents on behalf of an organisation	payee
The person or organisation to whom the cheque is written	stub
A written instruction to transfer a specified sum of money from one bank account to another.	monies
The part of a cheque or paying-in slip kept as a record of the transaction	signatory
The term used to describe different forms of payments and receipts including cash, cheques and direct bank transfers.	cheque

---

4 The cash book

4.1   The cash book

🔍 Definition

The Cash Book records receipts and payment made by cash, cheque, credit or debit card, or bank transfer.

One of the most important books used within a business is the cash book. There are various forms of cash book, a 'two column' and a 'three column' cash book.

A two column cash book records details of cash and bank transactions separately as shown here:

CASH BOOK

Date	Details	Bank	Cash	Date	Details	Bank	Cash
		£	£			£	£
		Receipts				Payments	

Notes

- The left hand side of the cash book represents the debit side – money received. Often the paying in slips, remittance advices received from customer and lists of receipts will be used to update this side of the cash book.

- The right hand side of the cash book represents the credit side – money paid out. Often the list of payments, direct debit/standing order schedules and cheque book stubs are used to update this side of the cash book.

- In practice, there is usually a column on both the debit and the credit side for the date.

- The details column describes the transactions – typically the name of the customer or supplier.

- The bank column on the debit side represents money received (by cheque or other bank payment) whereas the bank column on the credit side represents money paid (by cheque or other bank payment).

- The cash column on the debit side represents cash received whereas the cash column on the credit side represents cash paid out in respect of purchases or other expenses.

Some organisations keep separate cash books to record receipts and payments. These are known as the cash receipts book and cash payments book, respectively.

Test your understanding 6

Alba works in the accounts department at NB Solutions Ltd. She has been asked to complete a two column cash book by recording transactions from today.

For each of the following, indicate whether they should be on the left or right hand side of the Cash Book.

	Left / right
Money received	
Money paid out	
Credit	
Debit	
£220 cash to pay for catering at NB Solutions event	
Bank transfer from a one-off customer for £150	
Cheque from Miss B Craven for £232	
Cheque payable to How Two Ltd for £459	

4.2 The cash receipts book

Example

CASH RECEIPTS BOOK

Date	Details	Bank	VAT	Sales	Receivables	Bank Interest 'Received
		£	£	£	£	£
20/11	ABC Ltd.	1,350			1,350	
20/11	Cash Sale	660	110	550		
21/11	Interest	50				50
	Totals	**2,060**	**110**	**550**	**1,350**	**50**

In the example above, you can see that the company have used analysis columns to analyse the receipts so that they know what they represent. Most companies would do this in order to make it easier to perform the double-entry bookkeeping into the general ledger accounts. As mentioned previously, you will learn about this in the AAT Foundation Certificate qualification.

It is important to cross-cast your total figures at the bottom to ensure that what you have entered into the cash book is accurate.

Example

Using the previous example:

110 + 550 + 1,350 + 50 = 2,060

You can see from this example that by adding up the totals of the analysis columns, you can be confident that you have accurately recorded money received into the cash book.

Cross-casting helps to ensure that the figures being transferred into the accounts are accurate and free from misstatement. This contributes to the accurate calculation of the company's profit or loss figure.

Incorrect entries being recorded in any of the day books can lead to false information being reported to management.

For example, if you don't cross-cast your total figures in the sales day book to make sure that the total of the net and VAT columns equal the total of the receivables column, then the incorrect figures would be transferred to the accounts in the ledgers.

Not only would this mean wasting time trying to trace the figure before being able to correct it, there is also a danger that errors could go unnoticed.

If this was to happen, the sales figures within the management reports could be wrong. Management might think that the sales figures were down and could try to solve the issue, when in actual fact there was no issue in the first place. This is inefficient working and could result in loss of earnings for the company.

4.3 The cash payments book

> #### Example

CASH PAYMENTS BOOK

Date	Details	Bank	VAT	Stationery	Payables
		£	£	£	£
20/11	Lazza & Co	1,050			1,050
20/11	Stationery	420	70	350	
21/11	BNM	800			800
	Totals	**2,270**	**70**	**350**	**1,850**

The cash payments book works in exactly the same way as the cash receipts book, the only difference is that it is recording the monies paid out of the business.

Again, analysis columns may be used to analyse the expenditure to save time when posting the double-entry to the general ledger.

> #### Example

Using the previous example, cross casting to check for accuracy:

70 + 350 + 1,850 = 2,270

> #### Test your understanding 7

Jessica has been asked to match the following documents to the relevant book of prime entry.

Invoice to customer	Cash Payments Book
Credit note from supplier	Sales Day Book
Cash received from customer	Sales Returns Day Book
Invoice from supplier	Cash Receipts Book
Credit note to customer	Purchases Day Book
Cheque paid to supplier	Purchases Returns Day Book

📝 Test your understanding 8

Fill in the gaps below to complete the sentences. Choose from the Pick list provided.

The _____ is used to record invoices to customers.

The _____ is used to record credit notes to customers.

The _____ is used to record invoices from suppliers.

The _____ is used to record credit notes from suppliers.

The _____ is used to record monies received from customers.

The _____ is used to record monies paid to suppliers.

Pick List

Cash receipts book	Sales day book	Cash payments book
Purchases day book	Purchases returns day book	Sales returns day book

---

📝 Test your understanding 9

You work in the accounts department of Armistead & Co and one of your tasks is to sort the documents before they are entered in to the books of prime entry.

Armistead & Co

Ryan's Close
Lower Meltham
MT4 3SQ

Invoice no: 59870
Tax point: 1 July 2016

INVOICE

To: Pendleton Prisms
Stuart Street, Bristol, BR1 JQ8

Product	Quantity	Price per unit	Total
Anti-rust bike chain	100	£3.99	£399.00
Chainset and cable kit	5	£25.00	£125.00
			£524.00
		VAT 20%	£104.80
		Total	**£628.80**
Payment terms: 15 days net			

The book of prime entry to be used is:

Test your understanding 10

You work in the accounts department of Foe & Co and one of your tasks is to sort the documents before they are entered in to the books of prime entry.

Foe & Co			
Middlebrow MI4 3SQ		Invoice no: 598 Tax point: 18 July 20X6	
Credit Note			
To: Fi and Fun **Rose Avenue, Cardiff, CT1 JQ8**			
Product	Quantity	Price per unit	Total
KBM15	1	£35.99	£35.99
		VAT 20%	£7.19
		Total	**£43.18**
Payment terms: 15 days net			

Which daybook should this document be entered in?

5 The petty cash book

5.1 What is petty cash?

Definition

Petty cash is the small amount of cash that most businesses hold in order to make small cash payments, such as payment for coffee and milk for the staff kitchen.

5.2 Petty cash box

Holding cash on business premises is a security risk and therefore it is important that the petty cash is secure. It should be kept in a locked petty cash box and usually this itself will be held in the safe.

Only the person responsible for the petty cash should have access to the petty cash box.

5.3 Payment of petty cash

Petty cash is usually reimbursed to employees who have already incurred a small cash expense on behalf of the business. These payments should be made for valid business expenses only.

For this reason, the petty cashier should pay out to the employee on receipt of an authorised petty cash voucher and, where appropriate, VAT receipt.

Definition

A **petty cash voucher** is an internal document that details the business expenditure that an employee has incurred out of his own money.

This voucher must be authorised by an appropriate person before any amounts can be paid to that employee out of the petty cash box.

A typical petty cash voucher is shown below.

PETTY CASH VOUCHER				
Authorised by F R Clarke	Received by L Kent		No	4173
Date	Description		Amount	
4 April 20X7	Train Fare		12	50
	Total		12	50

Signature of person authorising voucher

Signature of claimant

Sequential voucher number

Details of expenditure including the date and the nature of the expense

Total paid to employee

5.4 Maintaining petty cash records

The cashier, on receipt of the petty cash voucher should check that the receipt is genuine and that the voucher amounts add up to the total. Once the petty cash vouchers have been received, checked, authorised and the employee reimbursed, the details are recorded in the petty cash book.

5.5 Writing up the petty cash book

The petty cash book is normally set out as a large ledger account with a small receipts side and a larger analysed payments side.

A typical petty cash book is set out below.

> **Example**

Receipts			Payments							
Date	Narrative	Total	Date	Narrative	Voucher no	Total	Postage	Cleaning	Tea & Coffee	VAT
						£	£	£	£	£
1 Nov	Bal b/f	35.50								
1 Nov	Bank	114.50	1 Nov	ASDA	58	23.50			23.50	
			2 Nov	Post Office Ltd	59	29.50	29.50			
			2 Nov	Cleaning materials	60	15.07		12.56		2.51
			3 Nov	Postage	61	16.19	16.19			

When cash is paid into the petty cash book it will be recorded on the receipts side (debit side) of the petty cash book.

Each petty cash voucher will then in turn be written up in the petty cash book on the payments (credit) side.

To ensure that no vouchers have been mislaid, petty cash vouchers are pre-numbered sequentially.

Each voucher is then entered into the petty cash book in the correct order, with each item of expenditure being recorded in the correct expense analysis column.

The receipts side of the petty cash book only requires one column, as the only receipt into the petty cash box is the regular payment of cash drawn out of the bank account to top up the tin.

From the example of a typical petty cash book (above), we can see that the balance brought forward was £35.50. This means that at the beginning of November, there was £35.50 in the tin. The petty cash has then been restored up to £150 by paying in an additional £114.50 which was drawn out of the bank and placed in the tin.

Payments out of the petty cash box will be for a variety of different types of expense and an analysis column is required for each type of expense in

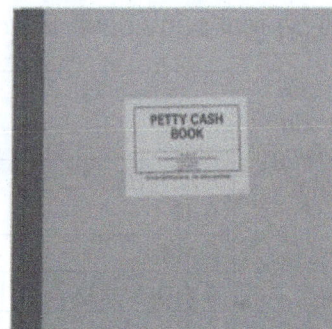

the same way as the cash payments book is analysed. The example (above) has split the expenses into postage, cleaning, tea & coffee and sundry expenses. Note that a column is also required for VAT, if a petty cash expense includes VAT this must also be analysed out.

5.6   Procedure for balancing the petty cash book

An organisation needs to know how much it has spent, and on what. In order to gain that information a balance of the petty cash book needs to be calculated:

This is done as follows:

Step 1   Total both the debit and the credit side of the petty cash book and make a note of each total.

Step 2   Insert the higher of the two totals as the total on both sides of the petty cash book leaving a line beneath the final entry on each side of the cash book.

Step 3   On the side with the smaller total insert the figure needed to make this column add up to the total. Call this figure the balance carried down (or 'Bal c/d' as an abbreviation).

Step 4   On the opposite side of the petty cash book, below the total insert this same figure and call it the balance brought down (or 'Bal b/d' as an abbreviation).

Here is an example of this method.

📖 Case study

The petty cash book of How Two Ltd. has the following entries:

Petty Cash Book				
	Debit			Credit
	£			£
Balance b/d	100	Tea & Coffee		5
Bank	100	Postage		10
		Taxi Fare		25

Calculate the balance on the account and bring the balance down as a single amount.

Step 1   Total both sides of the account and make a note of the totals. (Note that these totals that are asterisked below would not normally be written into the ledger account itself.)

Petty Cash Book			
	Debit		Credit
	£		£
Balance b/d	100	Tea & Coffee	5
Bank	100	Postage	10
		Taxi Fare	25
*Sub-total debits**	200	*Sub-total credits**	40

Step 2   Insert the higher total as the total of both sides.

Petty Cash Book			
	Debit		Credit
	£		£
Balance b/d	100	Tea & Coffee	5
Bank	100	Postage	10
		Taxi Fare	25
*Sub-total debits**	200	*Sub-total credits**	40
Total	200	Total	200

Step 3   Insert a balancing figure on the side of the account with the lower sub-total so that both sides total the same. This is referred to as the 'balance carried down' or 'bal c/d' for short.

Petty Cash Book			
	Debit		Credit
	£		£
Balance b/d	100	Tea & Coffee	5
Bank	100	Postage	10
		Taxi Fare	25
		Balance c/d	160
*Sub-total debits**	200	*Sub-total credits**	40
Total	200	Total	200

Step 4 Insert the balance carried down figure beneath the total on the other side of the account. This is referred to as 'bal b/d' for short.

Petty Cash Book				
	Debit			Credit
	£			£
Balance b/d	100	Tea & Coffee		5
Bank	100	Postage		10
		Taxi Fare		25
		Balance c/d		160
	———			———
Sub-total debits*	200	*Sub-total credits**		40
	———			———
Total	200	Total		200
	———			———
Balance b/d	160			

The closing balance carried down at the end of the period is also the opening balance brought down at the start of the next period. This opening balance remains in the account as the starting position and any further transactions are then added into the account. In this case the balance brought down is a debit balance as there is money in the bank account making it an asset.

🔍 Test your understanding 11

A business has just started to run a petty cash system with an amount of £100. £100 is withdrawn from the bank account and paid into the petty cash box on *3* April 20X7.

During the first week the following authorised petty cash vouchers were paid.

You are required to record these transactions in the petty cash book and total the columns appropriately. How much (if anything) would be left in the cash tin?

PETTY CASH VOUCHER

Authorised by T Smedley	Received by P Lannall	No		0001
Date	Description		Amount	
3 April 20X7	Tea/coffee/milk		4	73
	Total		4	73

PETTY CASH VOUCHER

Authorised by T Smedley	Received by R Sellers	No		0002
Date	Description		Amount	
3 April 20X7	Train fare		14	90
	Total		14	90

PETTY CASH VOUCHER

Authorised by T Smedley	Received by F Dorne	No		0003
Date	Description		Amount	
4 April 20X7	Stationery		4	00
	VAT		0	80
	Total		4	80

PETTY CASH VOUCHER

Authorised by T Smedley	Received by P Dent	No	0004
Date	Description	Amount	
5 April 20X7	Postage costs	16	35
	Total	16	35

PETTY CASH VOUCHER

Authorised by T Smedley	Received by H Polly	No	0005
Date	Description	Amount	
7 April 20X7	Train fare	15	30
	Total	15	30

PETTY CASH VOUCHER

Authorised by T Smedley	Received by P Lannall	No	0006
Date	Description	Amount	
8 April 20X7	Milk/biscuits	3	85
	Total	3	85

Answer

Petty cash book

Receipts			Payments								
Date	Narrative	Total	Date	Narrative	Voucher no	Total	Postage	Travel	Tea & coffee	Sundry	VAT
20X7		£	20X7			£	£	£	£	£	£

6 Batch control

6.1 Batch processing

A busy accounts office will need to record a lot of transactions and it is important that all the information is entered quickly and accurately into the correct book of prime entry.

Batch processing is a method of entering batches of similar transactions all together rather than individually. Using this method, all customer invoices, credit notes and receipts and all supplier invoices, credit notes and receipts will be sorted into separate piles before being entered into the relevant book of prime entry.

6.2 Benefits of batch processing

Batch processing will help to save time as it means that accounting staff can concentrate on one task at a time can be rather than swapping between different documents and books of prime entry. By focusing on one task at a time, it also means that fewer mistakes will be made.

Cheques and cash paid listings can be used to quickly record all the money paid out by the organisation each day. The total amount is then entered into the cash payments book.

Cheques and cash received listings can be used to record all the money received out by the organisation each day. The total amount is then entered into the cash receipts book.

Test your understanding 12

Complete the two sentences below with the correct options.

Batch processing is a method of processing financial documents [all together/individually] rather than [all together/individually].

Cheques and cash paid into the organisation can be listed on a [cheques and cash paid/cheques and cash received] listing before entering into the [cash payments book/cash receipts book].

This is an example of [batch processing/invoice processing] and means that [more/fewer] mistakes will be made.

---

7 Summary and further questions

In this chapter you learnt about the different day books used to keep of a record of the documents used in accounting transactions.

You should now understand which day books should be used for different transactions in the sales and purchasing processes. We have also shown how batch control can help accounting professionals to process information efficiently and effectively.

Let us now return to the How Two Ltd case study to apply this knowledge in context.

Case study activity 17

Jessica has been asked to set up the following payments. For each one indicate the best method of payment from the pick list provided.

Payment	Payment method
The telephone bill for calls and line rental for the Manchester office, for which the statement is paid in full on 15th of each month.	
A fixed monthly fee of £3,750, paid on 1st of each month, to Platinum Property Management for rent of the Liverpool offices.	
An urgent payment for £75 to a local contractor who is performing decorating and maintenance work in Reading, but will not work until paid.	
A refund to a small business who placed an order in error and do not have account terms with How Two Ltd. They have written to request the refund.	

Pick list

Cheque

Faster payment bank transfer

Direct debit

Standing order

Case study activity 18

Jessica has received the following three cheques in the week ended 20 November 20X7. Today is 20 November 20X7.

Are the cheques valid? Jessica needs to explain to her manager why easy is either suitable or unsuitable to take to the bank.

Cheque A

ABC Bank PLC	Date: 20th November, 2016
Payee: *How Two Ltd*	
	320.00
Three hundred and twenty pounds only	M Salinger
	M Salinger

CHEQUE NO	SORT CODE	ACCOUNT NO
00073	27-60-85	5921434

Cheque B

Plunketts Bank, Wiston	Date: 18th November, 2017
Payee: *How Two Ltd*	
	60.99
Sixty pounds & eighty-nine pence only	V Rogers, VCR Ltd
	Vic Rogers

CHEQUE NO	SORT CODE	ACCOUNT NO
02312	56-22-99	7421232

Cheque C

Royston Bank Ltd	Date: 16th November, 2017
Payee: *NB Solutions Ltd*	
	406.00
Four hundred and six pounds only	on behalf of N B Solutions Ltd
	O Smart

CHEQUE NO	SORT CODE	ACCOUNT NO
621001	40-08-09	6174931

Case study activity 19

Jessica has been asked to record the following receipts and payments into the cash book:

Receipts:

Cash sale 2nd November £100.

Cash sale 3rd November £80.

Cheque from IT Geeks on the 3rd November £550.

Cheque from NB Solutions on the 4th November £225.

Payments:

Cash purchase on the 2nd November £50.

Cheque paid to MMC Ltd. on the 3rd November £450.

Cheque paid to RBC Plc. On the 4th November £340.

Cash purchase on the 5th November £65.

Cash Book					
Date	Details	Amount	Date	Details	Amount

Case study activity 20

Jessica has been asked to enter the invoice below into the sales day book.

How Two Ltd

1 Baker Street
London
WC1 8QT

Invoice no: 5698
Tax point: 26 Nov 2017

INVOICE

To: G Thomas (A/C Ref TH02)
5 Holland Crescent, Chesham CA2 3HU

Product	Quantity	Price per unit	Total
Goods (Deluxe Laptop Case)	5	£50.12	£250.60
		VAT 20%	£50.12
		Total	£300.72
Payment terms: 30 days net			

Complete the Sales Day Book below with the correct information:

Date	Customer	Reference	Invoice No	Total £	VAT £	Net £

Case study activity 21

Jessica works for How Two Ltd. Given the document below, which day book should Jessica enter this document into?

King & Co

Highbrow
HI4 3SQ

Invoice no: 2867
Tax point: 18 June 20X6

Invoice

To: How Two Ltd
1 Baker Street, London WC1 8QT

Product	Quantity	Price per unit	Total
Item 5	10	£35.50	£355.00
		VAT 20%	£71.00
		Total	£426.00
Payment terms: 15 days net			

Case study activity 22

Jessica has been asked to send a cheque to a supplier (MMC Direct) for the payment of recent orders.

Which daybook should the amount be listed in?

Case study activity 23

Jessica needs to sort the documents received by How Two Ltd this week before they are entered in to the correct books of prime entry.

Which book of prime entry should be used for the following document?

Drake Kelleher Manufacturing

Unit 4 Appletree Industrial Estate
Merthyr Tydfil
CA99 9ZZ

Credit Note no:
05876
Tax point: 16 July 2016

CREDIT NOTE

To: How Two Ltd
1 Baker Street, London WC1 8QT

Product	Quantity	Price per unit (£)	Total (£)
Packing cases	4	5.00	20.00
		VAT 20%	4.00
		Total	24.00
Payment terms: 30 days net			

Case study activity 24

Jessica has been asked to record the following transactions into the petty cash book and balance it off:

1/11 Opening Balance £50

Receipts:

1/11 Top up from the bank £150

Payments:

2/11 Rail fare £15

3/11 Taxi fare £25

4/11 Postage £25

Petty Cash Book					
Date	Details	Amount	Date	Details	Amount

Answers to chapter activities

📝 Test your understanding 1

Date: 19/11/17	ABC Bank plc Manchester	£50 notes	
		£20 notes	60.00
		£10 notes	150.00
	Account How Two Ltd	£5 notes	100.00
		£2 coin	
		£1 coin	25.00
No of cheques: 2	Paid in by *J Howard*	Other coin	6.00
		Total cash	341.00
	Sort Code Account No	Cheques	2250.00
	25-22-78 30087251	Total £	2591.00

📝 Test your understanding 2

The paying-in slip must be dated and signed so that the bank cashier can contact the person who paid in the money in to the bank, in case there are any queries.

📝 Test your understanding 3

Cheque A

The amount needs to be included, in numbers – in this case 500.00.

ABC Bank PLC	Date: 29th November, 2017
Payee: *NB Solutions Ltd*	
	500.00
Five hundred pounds ONLY	on behalf of How Two Ltd
	J Howard

CHEQUE NO	SORT CODE	ACCOUNT NO
04312	25-22-78	30087251

Cheque B

The amount needs to be included in written form.

ABC Bank PLC	Date: 29th November, 2017
Payee: *Armistead & Co*	
Two hundred and fifty pounds and 50p	250.50 on behalf of How Two Ltd *J Howard*

CHEQUE NO	SORT CODE	ACCOUNT NO
04313	25-22-78	30087251

Cheque C

The date needs to be included, to state the day, month and year.

ABC Bank PLC	Date: **29th November, 2017**
Payee: *Mr P Sagan*	
Twenty five pounds and 20p only	25.20 on behalf of How Two Ltd *J Howard*

CHEQUE NO	SORT CODE	ACCOUNT NO
04314	25-22-78	30087251

Test your understanding 4

The statement is false.

Cheques can only be signed by authorised signatories.

Test your understanding 5

A person who are authorised to sign documents on behalf of an organisation

The person or organisation to whom the cheque is written

A written instruction to transfer a specified sum of money from one bank account to another.

The part of a cheque or paying-in slip kept as a record of the transaction

The term used to describe different forms of payments and receipts including cash, cheques and direct bank transfers.

payee

stub

monies

signatory

cheque

Test your understanding 6

	Left / right
Money received	Left
Money paid out	Right
Credit	Right
Debit	Left
£220 cash to pay for catering at NB Solutions event	Right
Bank transfer from a one-off customer for £150	Left
Cheque from Miss B Craven for £232	Left
Cheque payable to How Two Ltd for £459	Right

Test your understanding 7

Invoice to customer	=	Sales Day Book
Credit note from supplier	=	Purchase Returns Day Book
Cash received from customer	=	Cash Receipts Book
Invoice from supplier	=	Purchases Day Book
Credit note to customer	=	Sales Returns Day Book
Cheque paid to supplier	=	Cash Payments Book

Test your understanding 8

The **Sales day book** is used to record invoices to customers.

The **Sales returns day book** is used to record credit notes to customers.

The **Purchases day book** is used to record invoices from suppliers.

The **Purchases returns day book** is used to record credit notes from suppliers.

The **Cash receipts book** is used to record monies received from customers.

The **Cash payments book** is used to record monies paid to suppliers.

Test your understanding 9

You are dealing with documents for Armistead & Co. This invoice is **to** Pendleton Prisms, so they must be the customer.

Therefore, this is a customer invoice and should be entered into the sales day book.

Test your understanding 10

You are dealing with documents for Foe & Co. This credit note is **to** Fi and Fun, so they must be the customer.

Therefore, this is a credit note sent to a customer and should be entered into the sales returns day book.

KAPLAN PUBLISHING

Test your understanding 11

Petty cash book										
Receipts			**Payments**							
Date	Narrative	Total	Date	Narrative	Voucher no	Total	Postage	Travel	Tea & coffee	Sundry	VAT
20X1		£	20X1			£	£	£	£	£	£
03/04	Cash	100.00	03/04	Tea/coffee	0001	4.73			4.73		
			03/04	Train fare	0002	14.90		14.90			
			04/04	Stationery	0003	4.80				4.00	0.80
			05/04	Postage	0004	16.35	16.35				
			07/04	Train fare	0005	15.30		15.30			
			08/04	Milk/biscuits	0006	3.85			3.85		
						59.93	16.35	30.20	8.58	4.00	0.80

There would be £40.07 left in the tin (£100 - £59.93).

Test your understanding 12

Batch processing is a method of processing financial documents [**all together**] rather than [**individually**].

Cheques and cash paid into the organisation can be listed on a [**cheques and cash received listing**] before entering into the [**cash receipts book**].

This is an example of [**batch processing**] and means that [**fewer**] mistakes will be made.

Case study activity 17

Payment	Payment method
The telephone bill for calls and line rental for the Manchester office, for which the statement is paid in full on 15th of each month.	Direct debit
A fixed monthly fee of £3,750, paid on 1st of each month, to Platinum Property Management for rent of the Liverpool offices.	Standing order
An urgent payment for £75 to a local contractor who is performing decorating and maintenance work in Reading, but will not work until paid.	Faster payment bank transfer
A refund to a small business who placed an order in error and do not have account terms with How Two Ltd. They have written to request the refund.	Cheque

Case study activity 18

Cheque A – the date is incorrect (2016 not 2017), making the cheque invalid

Cheque B – the written value is £60.89 whereas the numerical value of the cheque is £60.99 – these amounts do not match so the cheque is invalid

Cheque C – the cheque is actually made payable to the payer (NB Solutions) rather than the payee. Therefore as the payee is not How Two Ltd, the cheque is not valid.

Case study activity 19

Cash Book					
Date	Details	Amount	Date	Details	Amount
2/11	Cash sale	100	2/11	Cash purchase	50
3/11	Cash sale	80	3/11	MMC Ltd.	450
3/11	IT Geeks	550	4/11	RBC Plc.	340
4/11	NB Solutions	225	5/11	Cash purchase	65

Case study activity 20

Date	Customer	Reference	Invoice No	Total £	VAT £	Net £
26 Nov 2017	G Thomas	TH02	5698	300.72	50.12	250.60

Case study activity 21

This invoice is sent from King and Co who must be the supplier of the goods. Therefore, this is an invoice received by How Two Ltd from a supplier and should be entered into the **purchases day book.**

Case study activity 22

This is a payment from How Two Ltd and should therefore be listed in the **cash payments book.**

Case study activity 23

Jessica is dealing with documents for How Two Ltd. This credit note is **from** Drake Kelleher Manufacturing, so they must be the supplier.

Therefore, this is a supplier credit note and should be entered in the **purchases returns day book.**

Case study activity 24

Petty Cash Book					
Date	Details	Amount	Date	Details	Amount
1/11	Opening Balance	50	2/11	Rail fare	15
1/11	Bank	150	3/11	Taxi fare	25
			4/11	Postage	25
			30/11	Bal c/d	135
	Total	200		Total	200
1/12	Bal b/d	135			

Bookkeeping basics

6

Introduction

This chapter covers the basics of bookkeeping within an organisation, providing an overview of the two main forms of bookkeeping: single entry and double entry bookkeeping.

By the end of the chapter, we will have established what single entry bookkeeping entails and when it might be used. We will then look at the basics of the all-important double entry bookkeeping, and what it represents.

KNOWLEDGE	CONTENTS
Understand financial transactions 2.3 The dual effect of transactions	1 Single and double entry bookkeeping 2 Debit and credit entries 3 Summary and further questions

1 Single and double entry bookkeeping

1.1 Case study: an introduction

📖 Case study

Jessica has a good knowledge of business documents and the books of prime entry used to record them.

As she has now taken on the role of junior bookkeeper, she now needs to look at the basics of bookkeeping within an organisation.

She is aware of the terms single entry and double entry bookkeeping, but needs to understand what these concepts mean and how to use them in practice. She needs to learn how each may be used and applied within an organisation's record keeping system.

1.2 Single entry bookkeeping

Many small businesses, particularly sole traders, are cash based, or do not have many transactions to record. For this reason the owner will often only use a cash book or spreadsheet to record the income and expenditure of the business.

	A	B
1	Cstd	Sstd
2	0.000	0.00
3	0.100	12.36
4	0.200	24.83
5	0.300	35.91
6	0.400	48.79
7	0.500	60.42

The spreadsheet will often have columns analysed by type. The cash book may not.

It is quicker and easier for the owner to record the transactions this way, but the records are incomplete, and will have to be reconstructed in order to work out the taxable profit.

1.3 Double entry bookkeeping

Most organisations use double entry bookkeeping to record the financial transactions of the business.

Due to the large volume of transactions (and therefore the increased chance of error), the process is divided into three parts.

a) The transactions are first recorded in a book of prime (first) entry, also referred to as "day books".

b) The second part is the general ledger itself where the double entry takes place

c)   The third part is, depending on the transaction, the sales ledger or purchase ledger which contains the individual customer and supplier accounts.   (These ledgers are also known as the subsidiary (sales/purchase) ledger.

The books of prime entry have already been addressed earlier in this book. Next in the process is the double entry. For the purpose of your assessment you don't need to be able to perform double-entry bookkeeping as this will be covered comprehensively in the AAT Foundation Certificate, but you do need to understand the principle of it.

Double-entry bookkeeping is based upon the principle of the dual effect.

1.4   The dual effect principle

We have already looked at the basic bookkeeping terminology and you should now be able to classify accounting items under the headings of assets, liabilities, income or expenditure. Each of these items are recorded into the bookkeeping system via double-entry. As double-entry is based upon the principle of the dual effect, it is important that you understand what it is and how this impacts the assets, liabilities, income or expenses of the business.

The dual effect states that every transaction has two financial effects.

(a)   If, for example, you spend £2,000 on a car and pay for it by a cheque, you will have £2,000 less money in the bank, but you will also have acquired an asset worth £2,000.

This can be viewed as:

Gained: a £2,000 car

Lost: £2,000 in cash.

The accounting terms used for this transaction are: **debit** and **credit**.

In the above example, the **debit** is the gain of a car, the **credit** is the loss of the money.

Using the accounting terminology, look at the example below:

(b)   If you buy from a supplier £100 of goods and send him a cheque for that amount, you will gain £100 worth of goods, but you will have £100 less money in the bank.

Debit   £100 of goods

Credit   £100 from the bank account

At first it can seem difficult, but break the transaction into two parts.

Ask:

*   What did I get?

*   What did I lose?

Example

	Debit (gain)	Credit (loss)
a) Purchases goods for resale, paid £800.	Purchases	Bank
b) Pays rent for use of office of £500.	Rent	Bank
c) Buys a van, cost £2,000.	Van	Bank
d) Sells some of the goods for £600.	Bank	Sales
e) Sells some more of the goods for £700.	Bank	Sales
f) Purchases goods for resale for £1,000.	Purchases	Bank
g) Buys stationery for £200.	Stationery	Bank

Explanation for the above example follows:

a)   Gains goods to sell on, loses £800 of money from bank account

b)   Gains office space, but loses £500 of money from bank account

c)   Gains a van, but loses £2,000 of money from bank account

d)   Gains £600, which is paid into bank account, but loses some of the goods previously bought

e)   Gains some money, £700, but more goods go out the door

f)   Gains some more goods to sell on, but spends (loses) £1,000 from bank account

g)   Gains some stationery to write on, but loses £200 from bank account

Test your understanding 1

Jessica has been presented with the following cash transactions made by How Two Ltd. She has been asked how the accounts will be affected with regards to debits and credits.

State which account will be debited and which will be credited.

	Debit (gain)	Credit (loss)
Purchases goods for resale for £700.		
Customer entertainment £300 for product launch.		
Purchases three computers for £3,000.		
Sells goods for £1,500.		
Purchases goods for resale for £1,200.		
Pays telephone bill of £600.		
Receives telephone bill rebate of £200.		
Purchases stationery for £157.		

2 Debit and credit entries

2.1 Debit and credit entries

We need to appreciate the effect a debit or a credit entry will have.

Ledger account	
A **debit entry** represents:	A **credit entry** represents:
• An increase in the value of an asset;	• A decrease in the value of an asset;
• A decrease in the value of a liability; or	• An increase in the value of a liability; or
• An increase to an item of expenditure	• An increase to an item of income (revenue)
• A decrease to an item of income	• A decrease to an item of expense.

2.2 DEAD CLIC

The mnemonic DEAD CLIC may help to remind you of which side the account balances should be.

Notice that some transactions are for cash (immediate payment) and some are credit transactions (payment will be made at a later date).

DEAD	CLIC
Debits:	**Credits:**
Expenses	**L**iabilities
Assets	**I**ncome
Drawings	**C**apital

Definitions

Capital is an amount of money that the owner of a business puts in to start it up. Essentially the business owes that money back to the owner and therefor it is classed as a **liability** of the business.

Drawings is an amount of money that is taken out of the business by the owner of the business for their own personal use. Essentially the owner owes that money back to the business and therefore they are classed as an asset to the business.

📖 **Case study**

Jessica is receiving some training from one of her colleagues who is keen to help her progress within her role. They are looking a little further into debits and credits and this is the information that Jessica was given:

Notice that some transactions are for cash (immediate) and some are for credit. Credit transactions mean that money is owed to the business by a credit customer (a receivable – an asset) or that the business owes money to a supplier (a payable – a liability).

Similarly, if a credit customer returns goods, you will decrease your asset (the receivable) because they don't owe you as much money as they did originally. You do this by crediting your receivables and debiting your sales returns account.

This works in exactly the same way for returns to a supplier only the debit and credit entries are the opposite way around. For example, if you return goods to a supplier, you don't owe them as much money as you did originally, therefore you debit your payables to reduce the liability and credit your purchase returns.

		Debit	Credit
Nov 1	Started business with £3,000 in the bank	Bank	Capital
Nov 3	Bought goods for cash £850	Purchases	Cash
Nov 7	Bought goods on credit for £1,160	Purchases	Payables
Nov 10	Sold goods for cash £420	Cash	Sales
Nov 14	Returned goods to a supplier for £100	Payables	Purchase Returns
Nov 20	Paid a gas bill for £80 by direct debit	Gas	Bank
Nov 21	Returned goods to a supplier for £190	Payables	Purchase Returns
Nov 24	Sold goods to a credit customer for £550	Receivables	Sales
Nov 25	Paid a supplier £500 out of the bank	Payable	Bank
Nov 31	A credit customer has returned goods worth £80	Sales Returns	Receivables
Nov 31	Paid an electricity bill for £100 by direct debit	Electricity	Bank

Test your understanding 2

Jessica's colleague wishes to know whether Jessica has understood what they have just been talking about and has asked her to state whether the following would be a debit or credit entry:

	Debit Dr	Credit Cr
An increase in income		
An increase in capital		
A decrease in expenses		
A decrease in a liability		
A decrease in drawings		
An increase in assets		
An increase in expenses		
A decrease in capital		

Test your understanding 3

Would the following accounts be represented as debits or credits in the accounts?

	Debit Dr	Credit Cr
Purchases		
Gas		
Wages		
Payables		
Capital		
Receivables		
A bank overdraft		
A bank loan		
Purchases Returns		
Sales		

Test your understanding 4

What does DEADCLIC stand for?

D		C	
E		L	
A		I	
D		C	

3 Summary and further questions

In this chapter we have studied cash and credit transactions. It is important to always start with the bank account and remember that cash received is a debit in the bank account and cash paid out is a credit in the bank account. If you get that right then the rest really does fall into place.

You should now be able to distinguish between increases and decreases to accounts as a result of a range of accounting transactions.

You should also be aware of the definitions of assets, expenses and income and the debit or credit entries you would need to make in the accounts for these.

Let us return to the case study for further activities to test your understanding and see how this is applied to How Two Ltd.

Case study activity 25

Jessica has then been given a list of recent transactions for How Two Ltd. For each, she needs to state the accounts which would be debited and credited.

Complete the table below.

	Debit Dr	Credit Cr
Sold goods for £500 and the customer pays cash		
Paid a gas bill for £90 by direct debit		
Purchased goods from a credit supplier for £300		
Returned goods to a supplier for £50		
Withdrawn £250 from the bank for personal use		
Sold goods to a credit customer for £800		
A credit customer returns goods worth £150		
Paid wages of £300 via a faster payment		

Case study activity 26

Jessica is explaining the idea of debit and credit entries to the new apprentice at How Two Ltd.

Which of Jessica's following statements are true and which are false?

	True	False
An increase in expenses is a credit		
An increase in drawings is a debit		
An increase in liabilities is a credit		
A decrease in assets is a debit		
A decrease in income is a debit		
A decrease in capital is a debit		

Answers to chapter activities

Test your understanding 1

	Debit (gain)	Credit (loss)
Purchases goods for resale for £700.	Purchases	Bank
Customer entertainment £300 for product launch.	Entertainment	Bank
Purchases three computers for £3,000.	Computers	Bank
Sells goods for £1,500.	Bank	Sales
Purchases goods for resale for £1,200.	Purchases	Bank
Pays telephone bill of £600.	Telephone	Bank
Receives telephone bill rebate of £200.	Bank	Telephone
Purchases stationery for £157.	Stationery	Bank

Test your understanding 2

	Debit Dr	Credit Cr
An increase in income		✓
An increase in capital		✓
A decrease in expenses		✓
A decrease in a liability	✓	
A decrease in drawings		✓
An increase in assets	✓	
An increase in expenses	✓	
A decrease in capital	✓	

Test your understanding 3

	Debit Dr	Credit Cr
Purchases	✔	
Gas	✔	
Wages	✔	
Payables		✔
Capital		✔
Receivables	✔	
A bank overdraft		✔
A bank loan		✔
Purchases Returns		✔
Sales		✔

Test your understanding 4

Debit	Credit
Expenses	Liabilities
Assets	Income
Drawings	Capital

Case study activity 25

	Debit Dr	Credit Cr
Sold goods for £500 and the customer pays cash	Cash	Sales
Paid a gas bill for £90 by direct debit	Gas	Bank
Purchased goods from a credit supplier for £300	Purchases	Payables
Returned goods to a supplier for £50	Payables	Purchase Returns
Withdrawn £250 from the bank for personal use	Drawings	Bank
Sold goods to a credit customer for £800	Receivables	Sales
A credit customer returns goods worth £150	Sales Returns	Receivables
Paid wages of £300 via a faster payment	Wages	Bank

Case study activity 26

	True	False
An increase in expenses is a credit		✓
An increase in drawings is a debit	✓	
An increase in liabilities is a credit	✓	
A decrease in assets is a debit		✓
A decrease in income is a debit	✓	
A decrease in capital is a debit	✓	

Bank reconciliations

7

Introduction

Completion of this chapter will ensure we are able to correctly prepare the cash book, compare the entries in the cash book to details on the bank statement and then finally to prepare a bank reconciliation statement.

We will explore the concept of the bank reconciliation, producing an updated cash book using this knowledge.

KNOWLEDGE	CONTENTS
Process receipts and payments	1 Writing up the cash book
4.1 Enter receipts and payments into a cash book	2 Preparing the bank reconciliation statement
4.2 Use the cash book to calculate closing amounts of cash in hand and cash in the bank	3 Summary and further questions
4.3 Check the closing amount of cash in the bank against the closing balance on the bank statement	

1 Writing up the cash book

1.1 Case study: an introduction

📖 Case study

Jessica is now ready to undertake the biggest challenge to date in her career. Her manager wants her to get an insight into the bank reconciliation - this will form part of her role in the near future.

However, for data protection and confidentiality reasons, it would be inappropriate to allow Jessica access to genuine company records until she is qualified and experienced enough to take on this role. It would also be inappropriate to allow a trainee to work with genuine records due to the scope for errors occurring. This could cause complications for the accounting department as the tracing of errors can be extremely time consuming and can have a knock on effect on other work deadlines. Therefore, Jessica will be working with scenarios and figures that have been fictitiously created for training purposes.

On completion of the tasks set, Jessica will be able to show that she can prepare the cash book correctly. She will need to compare the entries in the cash book to the details on the bank statement.

Attention to detail and accuracy when comparing the records is paramount as Jessica will then need to prepare a bank reconciliation statement. All tasks that Jessica completes will be reviewed by her manager who will provide feedback on her performance.

1.2 Balancing the cash book

Most businesses will have a separate cash receipts book and a cash payments book which form part of the double entry system. If this form of record is used, the cash balance must be calculated from the opening balance at the beginning of the period, plus the receipts shown in the cash receipts book for the period and minus the payments shown in the cash payments book for the period.

The following brief calculation will enable us to find the balance on the cash book when separate receipts and payments book are maintained.

	£
Opening balance per the cash book	X
Add: Receipts in the period	X
Less: Payments in the period	(X)
Closing balance per the cash book	X

📖 Case study

Jessica is being introduced to the process of completing a bank reconciliation for How Two Ltd. She is receiving some training from one of her colleagues who presents her with the following scenario:

Suppose that the opening balance on the cash book is £358.72 on 1 June. During June the cash payments book shows that there were total payments made of £7,326.04 during the month of June and the cash receipts book shows receipts for the month of £8,132.76.

She asks Jessica: What is the closing balance on the cash book at the end of June?

Solution

		£
Opening balance at 1 June		358.72
Add:	Receipts for June	8,132.76
Less:	Payments for June	(7,326.04)
Balance at 30 June		1,165.44

✏️ Test your understanding 1

To check that Jessica has understood what she has just been told, she has been presented with the following scenario and asked to calculate the closing balance of the cash book:

The opening balance at 1 January in a business cash book was £673.42. During January payments totalled £6,419.37 and receipts totalled £6,488.20.

What is the closing balance on the cash book?

Test your understanding 2

Within her training pack, Jessica is given the following:

Below is a cash book that needs updating with the receipts provided:

	£
10 May BACS	6,200
25 May Bank interest	40
31 May BACS	460

She needs to enter the amounts into the cash book

Date	Details	£	Date	Chq	Details	£
1 May	Balance b/d	526	1 May			
6 May	Shaws	630	3 May	0041	Bills Farm	2,000
6 May	Andrew Ltd	880	3 May	0042	Cows Head	3,240
			5 May	0043	Adam Ant	840
			30 May	0044	Miles to Go	700
	INT	*40*			*BA*	*6200*
						460

Money IN   Money OUT

2 Preparing the bank reconciliation statement

2.1 Introduction

At regular intervals (normally at least once a month) the cashier must check that the cash book is correct by comparing the cash book with the bank statement.

2.2 Differences between the cash book and bank statement

At any date the balance shown on the bank statement is unlikely to agree with the balance in the cash book for two main reasons.

(a) **Items in the cash book not on the bank statement**

Certain items will have been entered in the cash book but will not appear on the bank statement at the time of the reconciliation. Examples are:

- Cheques received by the business and paid into the bank which have not yet appeared on the bank statement, due to the time lag of the clearing system. These are known as **outstanding lodgements** (can also be referred to as "uncleared lodgements").

- Cheques written by the business but which have not yet appeared on the bank statement, because the recipients have not yet paid them in, or the cheques are in the clearing system. These are known as **unpresented cheques**.

- Errors in the cash book (e.g. transposition of numbers, addition errors).

(b) **Items on the bank statement not in the cash book**

At the time of the bank reconciliation certain items will appear on the bank statement that have not yet been entered into the cash book. These can occur due to the cashier not being aware of the existence of these items until receiving the bank statements.

Examples are:

- Direct debit or standing order payments that are in the bank statement but have not yet been entered in the cash payments book.

- BACS or other receipts paid directly into the bank account by a customer that have not yet been entered in the cash received book.

- Bank charges or bank interest that are unknown until the bank statement has been received and therefore will not be in the cash book.

- Errors in the cash book that may only come to light when the cash book entries are compared to the bank statement.

- Returned cheques i.e. cheques paid in from a customer who does not have sufficient funds in his bank to 'honour' the cheque (see later in this chapter).

2.3 Procedure for balancing the cash book

An organisation needs to know how much it has spent, and on what. In order to gain that information a balance of the cash book needs to be calculated:

This is done as follows:

Step 1 Total both the debit and the credit side of the cash book and make a note of each total.

Step 2 Insert the higher of the two totals as the total on both sides of the ledger account leaving a line beneath the final entry on each side of the cash book.

Step 3 On the side with the smaller total insert the figure needed to make this column add up to the total. Call this figure the balance carried down (or 'Bal c/d' as an abbreviation).

Step 4 On the opposite side of the ledger account, below the total insert this same figure and call it the balance brought down (or 'Bal b/d' as an abbreviation).

An example of the method is shown on the following page, returning back to the case study.

📖 **Case study**

Within the training session, Jessica's colleague works through the following example with Jessica to demonstrate the process to be followed when balancing off the cash book.

The cash book of a business has the following entries:

Cash Book			
	Debit		Credit
	£		£
Capital	1,000	Purchases	200
Sales	300	Drawings	100
Sales	400	Rent	400
Capital	500	Stationery	300
Sales	800	Purchases	400

Calculate the balance on the account and bring the balance down as a single amount.

Step 1 Total both sides of the account and make a note of the totals. (Note that these totals that are asterisked below would not normally be written into the ledger account itself.)

Cash Book			
	Debit		Credit
	£		£
Capital	1,000	Purchases	200
Sales	300	Drawings	100
Sales	400	Rent	400
Capital	500	Stationery	300
Sales	800	Purchases	400
	———		———
Sub-total debits*	**3,000**	**Sub-total credits***	**1,400**

Debits IN | *Credits OUT*

Step 2   Insert the higher total as the total of both sides.

Cash Book			
	£		£
	Debit		Credit
Capital	1,000	Purchases	200
Sales	300	Drawings	100
Sales	400	Rent	400
Capital	500	Stationery	300
Sales	800	Purchases	400
	─────		─────
Sub-total debits*	**3,000**	**Sub-total credits***	**1,400**
	─────		─────
Total	**3,000**	**Total**	**3,000**
	─────		─────

Step 3   Insert a balancing figure on the side of the account with the lower sub-total. This is referred to as the 'balance carried down' or 'bal c/d' for short.

Cash Book			
	Debit		Credit
	£		£
Capital	1,000	Purchases	200
Sales	300	Drawings	100
Sales	400	Rent	400
Capital	500	Stationery	300
Sales	800	Purchases	400
	─────		─────
Sub-total debits*	**3,000**	**Sub-total credits***	**1,400**
		Bal c/d	**1,600**
	─────		─────
Total	**3,000**	**Total**	**3,000**
	─────		─────

Step 4   Insert the balance carried down figure beneath the total on the other side of the account. This is referred to as 'bal b/d' for short.

Cash Book				
	Debit			Credit
	£			£
Capital	1,000	Purchases		200
Sales	300	Drawings		100
Sales	400	Rent		400
Capital	500	Stationery		300
Sales	800	Purchases		400
	———			———
Sub-total debits*	**3,000**	**Sub-total credits***		**1,400**
		Bal c/d		**1,600**
	———			———
Total	**3,000**	**Total**		**3,000**
	———			———
Bal b/d	**1,600**			

1400

The closing balance carried down at the end of the period is also the opening balance brought down at the start of the next period. This opening balance remains in the account as the starting position and any further transactions are then added into the account. In this case the balance brought down is a debit balance as there is money in the bank account making it an asset.

Test your understanding 3

Jessica has now been given another scenario to work through to demonstrate her ability to accurately balance off a cash book.

She is given the cash book for the month of March below and is required to "balance off" the cash book.

Cash Book					
Date		£	Date		£
1 Mar	Capital	12,000	3 Mar	Purchases	3,000
7 Mar	Sales	5,000	15 Mar	Computer	2,400
19 Mar	Sales	2,000	20 Mar	Purchases	5,300
22 Mar	Sales	3,000	24 Mar	Rent	1,000
			28 Mar	Drawings	2,000
				Bal c/d	8300
Total		22,000	Total		2200
Bal b/d		8300			

IN   OUT

2.4   The bank reconciliation

> ### 🔍 Definition
>
> **A bank reconciliation** is simply a statement that explains the differences between the balance in the cash book and the balance on the bank statement at a particular date.

A bank reconciliation is produced by following a standard set of steps.

Step 1:   Compare the cash book and the bank statement for the relevant period and identify any differences between them.

You should begin with agreeing the opening balances on the bank statement and cash book so that you are aware of any prior period reconciling items that exist.

This is usually done by ticking in the cash book and bank statement items that appear in both the cash book and the bank statement. Any items left unticked therefore only appear in one place, either the cash book or the bank statement. We saw in section 2.2 above the reasons why this might occur.

Step 2:   Update the cash book for any items that appear on the bank statement that have not yet been entered into the cash book.

Tick these items in both the cash book and the bank statement once they are entered in the cash book.

At this stage there will be no unticked items on the bank statement.

(You clearly cannot enter on the bank statement items in the cash book that do not appear on the bank statement – the bank prepares the bank statement, not you. These items will either be unpresented cheques, outstanding lodgements or errors in the cash book – see 2.2 above.)

Step 3:   You then need to balance the cash book to calculate the updated figure which is more realistic as the cash book now contains information on automated receipts/payments that hadn't been recorded but that have actually been received or paid.

Step 4:   Prepare the bank reconciliation statement.

This will typically have the following layout:

Bank reconciliation as at 31.0X.200X

	£
Balance as per bank statement	X
Less unpresented cheques	(X)
Add outstanding lodgements	X
	──
Balance as per cash book	X
	──

Think for a moment to ensure you understand this layout.

We deduct the unpresented cheques (cheques already entered in the cash book but not yet on the bank statement), these will be obvious as they will be the payments left in the cash book unticked. We do this because when the recipient pays them into their bank, our bank balance will be reduced.

We add outstanding lodgements (cash received and already entered in the cash book), these again will be obvious because they will be receipts left in the cash book unticked. We do this because when they clear in our bank, they will increase the bank balance.

2.5   Debits and credits in bank statements

When comparing the cash book to the bank statement it is easy to get confused with debits and credits.

- When we pay money into the bank, we debit our cash book but the bank credits our account.

- This is because a debit in our cash book represents the increase in our asset 'cash'. For the bank, the situation is different: they will credit our account because they now owe us more money; in the bank's eyes we are a payable.

- When our account is overdrawn, we owe the bank money and consequently our cash book will show a credit balance. For the bank an overdraft is a debit balance because we owe them money and therefore from their perspective we are a receivable.

On the bank statement a credit is an amount of money paid into the account and a debit represents a payment. A bank statement shows the transactions from the bank's point of view rather than the business' point of view.

Note: For the purpose of your assessment you are not required to complete the bank reconciliation statement. You are required to compare the items on the bank statement with those in the cash book and identify which one's are missing from each. You will also need to be able to calculate the closing amount of the cash in the bank.

The bank reconciliation statement has been included within this chapter so that you get a good understanding of the whole process and so that you can see the reasoning behind the missing items. Bank reconciliation statements will be covered in depth in the AAT Foundation Certificate.

Example

On 30 April Tomasso's received the following bank statement as at 28 April.

Today's date is 30 April.

QC Bank
QC Street, London

To: Tomasso's		Account No 92836152		30 April 20x7
Date	**Details**	**Payments**	**Receipts**	**Balance**
20x7		£	£	£
2 April	Bal b/f			100
3 April	Cheque 101	55		45
4 April	Cheque 103	76		(31)
6 April	Bank Giro Credit		1,000	969
9 April	Cheque 105	43		926
10 April	Cheque 106	12		914
11 April	Cheque 107	98		816
21 April	Direct Debit RBC	100		716
22 April	Direct Debit OPO	150		566
23 April	Interest received		30	596
24 April	Bank charges	10		586
28 April	Bank Giro Credit DJA		250	836

The cash book at 28 April is shown below.

Date 20x7	Details	Bank £	Date 20x7	Cheque number	Details	Bank £
	Balance b/f	100	01 April	101	Alan & Co	55
06 April	Prance Dance Co.	1,000	02 April	102	Amber's	99
23 April	Interest received	30	02 April	103	Kiki & Company	76
23 April	Graham Interiors	2,000	05 April	104	Marta	140
25 April	Italia Design	900	06 April	105	Nina Ltd	43
			07 April	106	Willy Wink	12
			08 April	107	Xylophones	98

Firstly, we see that the opening balance is £100 per both the bank statement and the cash book. Secondly, we must tick off the items in the bank statement to the cash book.

The effect of this on the bank statement can be seen below.

Date	Details	Payments £	Receipts £	Balance £
2 April	Bal b/f			100
3 April	Cheque 101	✔55		45
4 April	Cheque 103	✔76		(31)
6 April	Bank Giro Credit		✔1,000	969
9 April	Cheque 105	✔43		926
10 April	Cheque 106	✔12		914
11 April	Cheque 107	✔98		816
21 April	Direct Debit RBC	100		716
22 April	Direct Debit OPO	150		566
23 April	Interest received		✔30	596
24 April	Bank charges	10		586
28 April	Bank Giro Credit DJA		250	836

This leaves 4 items unticked on the bank statement. These transactions need to be added to the cash book and the cash book can then be balanced off.

The cash book is updated for these on the following page.

Date 20x7	Details	Bank £	Date 20x7	Cheque number	Details	Bank £
	Balance b/d	100	01 April	101	Alan & Co	✓55
06 April	Prance Dance Co.	✓1,000	02 April	102	Amber's	99
23 April	Interest received	✓30	02 April	103	Kiki & Company	✓76
23 April	Graham Interiors	2,000	05 April	104	Marta	140
25 April	Italia Design	900	06 April	105	Nina Ltd	✓43
28 April	DJA	250	07 April	106	Willy Wink	✓12
			08 April	107	Xylophones	✓98
			21 April	–	DD – RBC	100
			22 April	–	DD – OPO	150
			24 April	–	Bank charges	10
			28 April	–	Balance c/d	3,497
		4,280				4,280
29 April	Balance b/d	3,497				

Once the cash book has been updated, there are 4 items unticked on the cash book.

These are the items that will go onto the bank reconciliation, as shown below.

Bank reconciliation statement as at 28 April	£
Balance per bank statement	836
Add:	
Name: Graham's Interior	2,000
Name: Italia Design	900
Total to add	2,900
Less:	
Name: Amber's	99
Name: Marta	140
Total to subtract	239
Balance as per cash book	3,497

The bank reconciliation statement proves that the difference between the balance on the bank statement and the balance on the cash book is due to outstanding lodgements and unpresented cheques.

Test your understanding 4

FELICITY HOWE BOUTIQUE

Below is the cash book (bank columns only) of Felicity Howe Boutique for the month of April 20x7 together with her bank statement for the same period.

CASH BOOK

20x7		£	20X7		£
1 Apr	Balance b/d	1,470	2 Apr	Cheque 101129	930
9 Apr	Sales	606	4 Apr	Cheque 101130	506
12 Apr	Sales	1,048	9 Apr	Cheque 101131	834
30 Apr	Sales	550	29 Apr	Cheque 101132	410
			30 Apr	Balance c/d	994
		3,674			3,674
1 May	Balance b/d	994			

BANK STATEMENT

NORBURY BANK PLC
Southborough Branch
In account with: Felicity Howe   Account no 34578900

20X7		Payments	Receipts	Balance
01-Apr	balance b/f.			1,470
02-Apr	Cheque No. 129	930		540
05-Apr	Cheque No. 130	506		34
09-Apr	Counter Credit		606	640
12-Apr	Cheque No. 131	834		-194
12-Apr	Counter Credit		1,048	854
16-Apr	STO Hamble Comms.	75		779
17-Apr	BACS - Honey Bee		948	1,727
18-Apr	BACS - Goldfish CC	534		1,193
25-Apr	Overdraft fee	125		1,068
29-Apr	BGC S. May		610	1,678

Required:

a. Bring up to date the Cash Book making any adjustments necessary

b. Update the Cash Book and bring the balance down

c. Prepare a bank reconciliation statement as at 30 April 20x7

3 Summary and further questions

In this chapter you have learnt how to compare items in the cash book with those on the bank statement. You have also been able to identify items that are on the bank statement that have not been entered into the cash. From here you have gone on to update the accounting records accordingly.

Within this chapter you have learnt how to carry out a bank reconciliation and have presented this in the form of a bank reconciliation statement. As mentioned earlier in the chapter, in your exam you **will not** be tested on the bank reconciliation statement however you will need to demonstrate the ability to carry out all other activities set out in this chapter.

Let us return to the How Two Ltd case study for further activities to test your understanding of the topics covered in the chapter.

Case study activity 27

Having gained considerable experience in the bookkeeping team at How Two Ltd, Jessica has been promoted and is preparing to complete her first bank reconciliations.

Before she does so, her manager wants to check that she fully understands the process. Jessica is given a list of statements and needs to decide whether each is true or false. Tick the correct box for each

Statement	True	False
An outstanding lodgement is a cheque that has been received by the business, paid into the bank, and has appeared on the bank statement		
An outstanding lodgement is a cheque that has been received by the business, paid into the bank, but has not yet appeared on the bank statement		
An unpresented cheque is one that has been written by the business but which has not yet appeared on the bank statement		
Direct debits that only show on the bank statement should be ignored		
Direct debits and standing orders that only show on the bank statement should be written into the cash book		
Bank charges are receipts to be entered into the cash book on the debit side		
Errors in the cash book may only come to light when the cash book entries are compared to the bank statement		

Case study activity 28

It is November 20X8. Having convinced her manager she is ready, Jessica has been promoted and is now responsible for How Two Ltd's bank reconciliations.

The cash book shows a debit balance of £204 on 30 November 20X8.

A comparison with the bank statements revealed the following:

		£
1	Cheques drawn but not presented	3,168
2	Amounts paid into the bank but not credited	723
3	Entries in the bank statements not recorded in the cash account	
	(i) Standing orders	35
	(ii) Interest on bank deposit account	18
	(iii) Bank charges	14
4	Balance on the bank statement at 30 November	2,618

Jessica needs to:

a) Show the appropriate adjustments required in the cash book of bringing down the correct balance at 30 November 20X8.

b) Prepare a bank reconciliation statement at that date.

Answers to chapter activities

Test your understanding 1

	£
Opening balance	673.42
Payments	(6,419.37)
Receipts	6,488.20
Closing balance	742.25

The closing balance is £742.25 cash surplus.

Test your understanding 2

Updated cash book:

Date	Details	£	Date	Chq	Details	£
1 May	Balance b/d	526				
6 May	Shaws	630	3 May	0041	Bills Farm	2,000
6 May	Andrew Ltd	880	3 May	0042	Cows Head	3,240
10 May	BACS	6,200	5 May	0043	Adam Ant	840
25 May	Bank Interest	40	30 May	0044	Miles to Go	700
31 May	BACS	460				
			31 May		Balance c/d	1,956
		8,736				8,736
1 June	Balance b/d	1,956				

KAPLAN PUBLISHING

Test your understanding 3

Cash Book

Date		£	Date		£
1 Mar	Capital	12,000	3 Mar	Purchases	3,000
7 Mar	Sales	5,000	15 Mar	Non-current asset	2,400
19 Mar	Sales	2,000	20 Mar	Purchases	5,300
22 Mar	Sales	3,000	24 Mar	Rent	1,000
			28 Mar	Drawings	2,000
			31 Mar	Balance c/d	8,300
		———			———
		22,000			22,000
		———			———
1 Apr	Balance b/d	8,300			

Test your understanding 4

a. Bring up to date the Cash Book making any adjustments necessary

CASH BOOK

20x7		£	20x7		£
1 Apr	Balance b/d	1,470✓	2 Apr	Cheque 101129	930✓
9 Apr	Sales	606✓	4 Apr	Cheque 101130	506✓
12 Apr	Sales	1,048✓	9 Apr	Cheque 101131	834✓
30 Apr	Sales	550	29 Apr	Cheque 101132	410
			30 Apr	Balance c/d	994
		3,674			3,674
1 May	Balance b/d	994✓			

BANK STATEMENT

20x7		Payments	Receipts	Balance
01 Apr	Balance b/f			1,470✓
02 Apr	Cheque 101129	930✓		540
05 Apr	Cheque 101130	506✓		34
09 Apr	Counter credit		606✓	640
12 Apr	Cheque 101131	834✓		(194)
12 Apr	Counter credit		1,048✓	854
16 Apr	STO Hamble Comms	75✓		779
17 Apr	BACS – Honey Bee		948✓	1,727
18 Apr	BACS – Goldfish CC	534✓		1,193
25 Apr	Overdraft fee	125✓		1,068
29 Apr	BGC S May		610✓	1,678

b. Update the Cash Book and bring the balance down

FELICITY HOWE BOUTIQUE

CASH BOOK

20x7 30 April			20x7		
	Balance b/d.	994.00✓			
	Honey Bee	948.00✓	16 April	Hamble Comms.	75.00✓
	S. May	610.00✓	18 April	Goldfish CC	534.00✓
			25 April	Bank charges	125.00✓
				Balance c/d.	1,818.00
		£ 2,552.00			£ 2,552.00
1 May	Balance b/d.	1,818.00			

c. Prepare a bank reconciliation statement as at 30 April 20x7

Felicity Howe Boutique Bank reconciliation statement as at 30 April	£
Balance per bank statement	1,678
Add:	
Name: Sales	550
Total to add	550
Less:	
Name: 101132	410
Total to subtract	410
Balance as per cash book	1,818

Case study activity 27

Statement	True	False
An outstanding lodgement is a cheque that has been received by the business, paid into the bank, and has appeared on the bank statement		✔
An outstanding lodgement is a cheque that has been received by the business, paid into the bank, but has not yet appeared on the bank statement	✔	
An unpresented cheque is one that has been written by the business but which has not yet appeared on the bank statement	✔	
Direct debits that only show on the bank statement should be ignored		✔
Direct debits and standing orders that only show on the bank statement should be written into the cash book	✔	
Bank charges are receipts to be entered into the cash book on the debit side		✔
Errors in the cash book may only come to light when the cash book entries are compared to the bank statement	✔	

📖 **Case study activity 28**

a)

Cash book			
	£		£
Balance b/d	204	Sundry accounts	
Interest on deposit account	18	Standing orders	35
		Bank charges	14
		Balance c/d	173
	————		————
	222		**222**
	————		————
Balance b/d	173		

b)

BANK RECONCILIATION STATEMENT AT 30 NOVEMBER 20X8

	£
Balance per bank statement	2,618
Add Outstanding lodgements	723
	————
	3,341
Less Unpresented cheques	(3,168)
	————
Balance per cash account	173
	————

Mock Assessment 1 – Access Award in Bookkeeping

Introduction

The following is a Mock Assessment to be attempted in exam conditions.

You should attempt and aim to complete EVERY task.

Read every task carefully to make sure you understand what is required.

Where the date is relevant, it is given in the task.

Both minus signs and brackets can be used to indicate negative numbers UNLESS task instructions say otherwise.

You must use a full stop to indicate a decimal point.

The assessment includes eight tasks.

Time allowed: 90 minutes

1 Mock Assessment Questions

Task 1 (7 marks)

a)   State whether the following are the responsibility of a bookkeeper within an organisation by putting a tick in the correct box.

	Yes	No
Entering sales invoices and credit notes onto the system	✓	
Maintaining the cash book	✓	
Approving salary increases for sales staff		✓

As a bookkeeper it is important to observe confidentiality.

b)   Show whether the following statement is true or false.

Statement	True	False
If a manager asks to see confidential information, you should let them see it		✓

c)   Complete the following sentence by selecting the most appropriate option from the pick list below.

Confidential information should be _____if you have to leave your desk.

Pick list

- kept in a locked drawer ✓
- hidden under the computer keyboard
- given to a colleague for safekeeping

d) State whether the following sentences are true or false by putting a tick in the relevant box.

Statement	True	False
Making an underpayment to a supplier is good for business as it will increase the profit figure.		✓
Spending time tracing and correcting errors in the bookkeeping system is good for business as it is a cost-effective way of ensuring information is accurate	✗	✓

Task 2 (11 marks)

a) Insert an item from the following list into the right hand column of the table below to identify the term described. You will not need to use all of the items.

Description	Term described
A customer who owes an organisation money	
A transaction when an organisation buys goods or services and pays its supplier immediately	
A transaction to purchase goods when payment is made a month later.	
An organisation that is owed money for goods or services supplied.	

Pick list

A cash sale   A cash purchase   A credit sale

A credit purchase   A receivable/debtor   A payable/creditor

b) Complete the sentence below by selecting the most appropriate option from the following list:

- equals
- is more than
- is less than

When expenditure _____ income this results in a loss.

c) Place a tick in the appropriate column of the table below to show whether each of the items listed is an example of an asset, a liability, income or expenditure.

You should not place more than one tick against each item.

Item	Asset	Liability	Income	Expenditure
Cash sales				
Rent				
Office computers				

d) Organisations issue and receive different documents when buying and selling goods.

Complete the sentences below by inserting the most appropriate option from the following pick list:

- a purchase order
- a receipt
- an invoice
- a statement of account
- a remittance advice
- a credit note

i) An organisation sends _____ listing the items returned to the customer and showing the amount refunded.

ii) An organisation sends _____ to a supplier listing the items it wishes to purchase.

iii) An organisation sends _____ to a supplier along with the payment with details of the transaction included in the payment.

Task 3 (11 marks)

Sunnyside Ltd. wish to purchase 12 x Hanging Baskets and 18 x Ceramic Plant Pots from Happydays PLC.

The list price of the Hanging Baskets is £17.90 and the list price of the Ceramic Plant Pots is £15.50. The last purchase order number used was PO1090.

Sunnyside Ltd. have agreed 10 day payment terms with Happydays PLC. VAT is charged at the standard rate of 20% and today's date is 28th November 20X7.

a)   Complete the following purchase order with the following information:

- Customer name

- Supplier name

- PO number

- Product pricing

- Net

- VAT

- Total

Purchase Order

Sunnyside Ltd

476 Laneside Road

Oxford

OX10 5WD

VAT Reg No. 397 8682 00

Tel No: 01346 572354

To: *Happydays PLC*

Date: 28/11/20X7

P.O. Number: *PO1091*

Wayside Business Park

Taunton

TN5 6NQ

Quantity	Description	Unit Price	Price
12	Hanging Baskets	17'90	214'80
18	Ceramic Plant Pots	15'50	279'00
		Net	493'80
		VAT	98'76
		Total	592'56

Payment terms agreed: 10 days

Task 4 (7 marks)

A supply of paper has been delivered to Alpha Ltd by Pixie Paper. The purchase order sent from Alpha Ltd, and the invoice from Pixie Paper, are shown below.

Alpha Ltd.
121 Baker St
Newcastle
NE1 7DJ

Purchase Order No. PO1792

To: Pixie Paper
Date: 5 Aug 20X7

Please supply 50 boxes of A4 paper product code 16257
Purchase price: £10 per box, plus VAT

Pixie Paper
24 Eden Terrace
Durham
DH9 7TE

VAT Registration No. 464 392 401

Invoice No. 1679

Alpha Ltd
121 Baker St
Newcastle
NE1 7DJ

9 Aug 20X7

50 boxes of A4 paper, product code 16257 @ £11 each

Net	£550
VAT	£110
Total	£660

Terms: 30 days net

Check the invoice against the purchase order and answer the following questions.

a) Which ONE of the following is a true statement relating to the invoice provided by Pixie Paper when checked against the purchase order? Tick the correct answer.

Statement	
The incorrect address has been used	
The incorrect product has been supplied	
The incorrect net price has been calculated	✓

b) What would be the net amount charged if the invoice was correct?

£

c) What would be the VAT amount charged if the invoice was correct?

£

d) What would be the total amount charged if the invoice was correct?

£

e) Based on the information provided, what action should be taken? Tick the most appropriate answer.

Action	
The invoice should be filed but not paid	
The invoice should be referred back to a supervisor	✓
The invoice should be paid	

Task 5 (12 marks)

Three sales credit notes have been partially entered into the relevant day book below:

GGD Ltd
117 Vinefield Place
Warminster
Kent WA1 1BB

Credit Note 552	**Date:1 Dec 20X7**
	£
250 products GUP @ £2.00	500.00
VAT @ 20%	100.00
Gross amount refunded	600.00

Terms: Net monthly account

Day Associates
2 London Road
Becksley
Kent BE7 9MN

Credit Note 35	**Date:10 Dec 20X7**
	£
24 products Y12 @ £5.75	138.00
VAT @ 20%	27.60
Gross amount refunded	165.60

Terms: Net monthly account

Cohen PLC
25 Main Road
Rexsome
Herefordshire HR2 6PS

Credit Note 1168	**Date:23 Dec 20X7**
	£
80 products Y12 @ £7.10	568.00
VAT @ 20%	113.60
Gross amount refunded	681.60

Terms: Net monthly account

---

a) Given this information:

    i) Enter the correct name of the day book in the space provided.

    ii) Complete the entries in the day book by inserting the missing figures for each of the credit notes.

    iii) Total the day book.

[_____] day book

Date 20XX	Details	Credit note number	Total £	VAT £	Net £
1 June	GGD Ltd	552	600	100.00	500.00
10 June	Day Associates	138	165.60	27.60	138
23 June	Cohen PLC	1168	681.60	113'60	568.00
	Totals		1,447.20	241.20	1,206

b) You recently started trading with a new supplier. Below is a list of transactions between you and the supplier for November 20X7.

Document Type	Total Amount (£)
Invoice	450.00 ✓
Credit Note	✓ 125.00
Invoice	324.50 ✓
Invoice	675.35 ✓
Remittance	325.00
Credit Note	✓ 121.00

Complete the following table to calculate how much you owe to the supplier at the end of November. You do not need to enter minus signs or brackets in your answer.

		£
Total of invoices		1,449.85
Total of credit notes	Add / Deduct	246
Remittance advice	Add / Deduct	325
Amount owed at the end of November		879.85

c)   Should the business record the amount owing to the supplier at the
      end of November as an asset or a liability?

┌─────────────────────────┐
│   │
└─────────────────────────┘

Task 6 (15 marks)

You are working on the payments side of the cash book. There are four
bank payments to record.

Cash Purchases Listing

Date	Paid to	Details	Net (£)	VAT (£)	Total (£)
2/12/X7	J Carroll	Cleaning	80.00	16.00	96.00
12/12/X7	Rymann	Stationery	42.50	8.50	51.00

Payments to trade payables

Date	Supplier	£
8/12/X7	ABS Ltd.	455.00
20/12/X7	PnP Express	525.60

Complete the payments side of the cash book shown below.

Enter details into the relevant columns, and enter figures to complete each
column.

Total each column and check your work by cross casting your figures.

Cash book extract – payments side

Date	Details	Bank (£)	VAT (£)	Trade payables (£)	Cleaning (£)	Stationery (£)
2/12/X7	J Carroll	96.00				
8/12/X7	ABS Ltd.					
12/12/X7	Rymann					
20/12/X7						
Totals						

Task 7 (8 marks)

You are working on the receipts side of the cash book. For this task you may ignore VAT.

The following cash sales were counted and put into the safe.

Date	Details	Total (£)
15/12/X7	Cash Sales	54.00

The following amounts were received from credit customers.

Date	Customer	Payment Type	Total (£)
12/12/X7	C Bradley & Co	Faster Payment	469.75
19/12/X7	Floortech Ltd.	Cheque	558.90

Complete the receipts side of the cash book shown below.

Enter details into the relevant columns, and enter figures to complete each column.

Total each column and check your answer by cross casting your figures.

Cash book extract – receipts side

Details	Bank (£)	Cash (£)	Trade Receivables (£)	Cash Sales (£)
C Bradley & Co	469.75		469.75	
Cash Sales				
Floortech Ltd.				
Totals				

Task 8 (9 marks)

You have the following information about cash in hand.

Date	Details	Amount (£)
30/11/X7	Amount counted at the end of the day	125.00
2/12/X7	Cash sales	225.00
4/12/X7	Paid for postage	25.00
6/12/X7	Paid a train fare	80.00
10/12/X7	Cash sales	154.00
15/12/X7	Cash sales	201.50
19/12/X7	Paid a taxi fare	18.50
21/12/X7	Paid the cleaner	50.00

a)   Complete the table to calculate the closing amount of cash in hand on the 21st December. You do not need to use minus signs or brackets in your answer.

Cash in hand	£
Opening amount on 1st December 20X7	125.00
Total receipts	
Total payments	
Closing amount on 21st December 20X7	

b) You have the following extract from the business bank statement.

Bank statement

Date 20XX	Details	Paid out £	Paid in £	Balance £
01 Dec	Balance b/d			4,550
03 Dec	Counter credit – S Callaghan		75	4,625
9 Dec	Counter credit – B Wadhurst		800	5,425
13 Dec	Faster Payment – Waterloo plc	120		5,305
14 Dec	Cheque – P Umpkin	951		4,354
19 Dec	Counter credit – S Top		115	4,469
20 Dec	Cheque – Simply Stationery		70	4,539
21 Dec	Cheque - Geordie Gas	180		4,359
26 Dec	BACS Receipt – H.I. Light		720	5,079
27 Dec	BACS Receipt – R Winder		99	5,178

What is the closing balance on the bank statement on 14th December?

c) You also have an extract from the cash book for December covering the same period of time.

Cash book

Details	Reference	Bank	Details	Reference	Bank
Balance b/d		4,550	P Umpkin	Cheque	951
S Callaghan	Counter credit	75	Waterloo plc	Faster Payment	120
B Wadhurst	Counter credit	800	Geordie Gas	Cheque	180
S Top	Counter credit	115	R Williams	Faster Payment	240
Simply Stationery	Cheque	70			
R Winder	BACS Receipt	99			

Compare the extracts from the bank statement and the cash book, and complete the following sentences:

		✔		
The item that is missing from the bank statement is….	a cheque			
	A counter credit		for an amount of	£
	A faster payment			
	A BACS payment			
	A BACS receipt			

		✔		
The item that is missing from the cash book is….	a cheque			
	a counter credit		for an amount of	£
	a faster payment			
	a BACS payment			
	a BACS receipt			

		✔	
The missing item will need to go on the….	receipts		side of the cash book.
	payments		

Mock Assessment 2 – Access Award in Bookkeeping

Introduction

The following is a Mock Assessment to be attempted in exam conditions.

You should attempt and aim to complete EVERY task.

Read every task carefully to make sure you understand what is required.

Where the date is relevant, it is given in the task.

Both minus signs and brackets can be used to indicate negative numbers UNLESS task instructions say otherwise.

You must use a full stop to indicate a decimal point.

The assessment includes eight tasks.

Time allowed: 90 minutes

1 Mock Assessment Questions

Task 1 (7 marks)

a) Show whether the following statements are true or false.

Statement	True	False
A bookkeeper is able to authorise all financial transactions		
A bookkeeper is responsible for preparing and checking financial documentation		

It is important to for a bookkeeper to observe confidentiality.

b) Show whether the following statement is true or false.

Statement	True	False
Information about staff wages should not be held on the computer because it is confidential information.		

c) Complete the following sentence by selecting the most appropriate option from the pick list below.

The addresses of all staff should be accessible to

_____.

Pick list

- all staff
- accounts department staff only
- authorised staff only

d) Complete the following sentence.

		✓
A bookkeeping error can result in...	authorisation of the purchase of an asset	
	duplicated payments to suppliers	

e)   A bookkeeper issued a sales invoice to a customer. The total was overstated by £250.

What effects might this overstatement have on the business?

		✓
This could result in the customer making an…	underpayment	
	overpayment	

f)   Complete the following sentence.

		✓	
The overstatement…	could		…affect the recorded profit of the business
	could not		

Task 2 (11 marks)

It is important to understand the terminology used when buying and selling goods for cash and on credit.

a) Insert an item from the following pick list into the right hand column of the table below to identify the term described. You will not need to use all of the items.

Description	Term described
A person or organisation who is owed money by the company for purchases made.	
A transaction to sell goods when the payment is made one month later.	

Pick list

A cash sale	A cash purchase	A credit sale
A credit purchase	A debtor/receivable	A creditor/payable

Organisations have assets, liabilities, income and expenditure.

b) Which of the following statements describes an item of expenditure? Place a tick in the appropriate box.

Statement	✔
Expenditure is the money paid to an organisation by customers.	
Expenditure is the money paid by an organisation to purchase goods and services	
Expenditure is the amount an organisation owes to others.	

c) Place a tick in the appropriate column of the table below to show whether each of the items listed is an example of an asset, a liability, income or expenditure.

Item	Asset	Liability	Income	Expenditure
Sales				
Vehicles				
Insurance				
Bank Loan				

d)   Organisations issue and receive different documents when buying and selling goods.

Complete the sentences by inserting the most appropriate option from the following pick list:

- a purchase order

- a receipt

- an invoice

- a statement of account

- a remittance advice

- a credit note

i)   An organisation sends _____ to a customer with details of items purchased, the amount owing and the terms of payment.

ii)   An organisation sends _____ to a creditor accompanying a payment, listing items included in that payment.

e)   A business receives a cheque from one of its credit customers.

Complete the following sentences to show the effects of this transaction.

	Select one	
It will….	increase	the amount recorded in the business bank account
	decrease	
It will	increase	the amount the business records as outstanding from their receivables
	decrease	

Task 3 (11 marks)

ABC Ltd. wish to purchase 10 x Product S123 and 15 x Product RC557.

The list price of product S123 is £10.99 and the list price for product RC557 is £12.50.

The last purchase order number used was PO12456. ABC Ltd. have agreed 30 day payment terms with XYZ Ltd. VAT is charged at the standard rate of 20% and today's date is 27th November 20X7.

a)   Complete the following purchase order with the following information:

- Customer name

- Supplier name

- PO number

- Product quantities/pricing

- Net

- VAT

- Total

Payment terms	**Purchase Order**	

123 High Street

Manchester

M23 1RD

VAT Reg No. 441 3898 00

Tel No: 0161 838 9921

To:

Sunnyside

Beach Business Park

LN1 5NQ

Date: 27/11/20X7

P.O. Number:

Quantity	Description	Unit Price	Price
	Product S123	10.99	
15	Product RC557		
		Net	
		VAT	
		Total	
Payment terms agreed:			

Task 4 (7 marks)

a) You work for ABC Ltd. You have a goods returned note and a purchases credit note. Check that the information entered on the credit note is correct. Mark all highlighted boxes with a tick or cross to show if they have been input accurately.

ABC Ltd.
123 High Street
Manchester
M23 1RD

VAT Registration No. 441 3898 00

Goods Returned Note

XYZ Ltd.
Sunnyside
Beach Business Park
LN1 5NQ

30 Nov 20X7

Description	Reason for return	Unit Price (£)	Quantity
S123	Damaged	10.99	2
RC557	The wrong size	12.50	1

XYZ Ltd.
Sunnyside
Beach Business Park
LN1 5NQ

VAT Registration No. 419 7020 00

Credit Note

ABC Ltd.
123 High Street
Manchester
M23 1RD

2 Dec 20X7

Description	Quantity	✓ / x	Unit Price (£)	✓ / x	Total	✓ / x
S123	1		19.09		19.09	
RC557	1		12.50		12.50	
				Net	31.59	
				VAT	6.31	
				Total	37.90	

b) Complete the following sentence.

		✓
Based on the information I have, I will…..	accept the credit note and input it onto the system	
	process the credit note but raise it with my supervisor as an issue	
	refer the credit note to my supervisor	

Task 5 (12 marks)

a) Three purchase invoices have been partially entered into the purchase day book.

GGD Ltd	
117 Vinefield Place	
Warminster	
Kent WA1 1BB	
Invoice 3575	**Date:21 October 20XX**
	£
70 units of SPLAT @ 12.75	892.50
VAT @ 20%	178.50
Total	1,071.00
Terms: Net monthly account	

Day Associates	
2 London Road	
Becksley	
Kent BE7 9MN	
Invoice 35	**Date:22 October 20XX**
	£
2400 units of AA12 @ £0.55	1,320.00
VAT @ 20%	264.00
Total	1,584.00
Terms: Net monthly account	

Cohen PLC
25 Main Road
Rexsome
Herefordshire HR2 6PS

Invoice 1164	Date:23 October 20XX
	£
40 units of Y12 @ £14.20	568.00
VAT @ 20%	113.60
Total	681.60
Terms: Net monthly account	

Using this information to:

i) Enter the correct name of the day book in the space provided.

ii) Complete the entries in the day book by inserting the missing figures for each of the invoices.

iii) Total the day book.

[   ] **day book**

Date 20XX	Details	Invoice	Total £	VAT £	Net £
1 June	GGD Ltd	3575		178.50	892.50
10 June	Day Associates	35	1,584.00		1,320.00
23 June	Cohen PLC	1164	681.60	113.60	
	Totals				

b) You recently started trading with a new customer. Below is a list of transactions between you and the customer for November 20X7.

Document Type	Total Amount (£)
Invoice	221.00
Credit Note	54.00
Invoice	556.96
Remittance	167.00
Invoice	339.50

Complete the following table to calculate how much is owed by the customer at the end of November. You do not need to enter minus signs or brackets in your answer.

		£
Total of invoices		
Credit note	Add / Deduct	
Remittance advice	Add / Deduct	
Amount owing at the end of November		

c)   Should the business record the amount owing from the customer at the end of November as an asset or a liability?

Task 6 (15 marks)

You are working on the payments side of the cash book. There are four bank payments to record.

Cash Purchases Listing

Date	Paid to	Details	Net (£)	VAT (£)	Total (£)
15/12/X7	Locksmiths r us	Repairs	25.00	5.00	30.00
22/12/X7	Paperchain Ltd.	Stationery	65.00	13.00	78.00

Payments to trade payables

Date	Supplier	£
18/12/X7	RMT Ltd.	238.00
24/12/X7	Caldwell Plc.	154.00

Complete the payments side of the cash book shown below.

Enter details into the relevant columns, and enter figures to complete each column.

Total each column and check your work by cross casting your figures.

Cash book extract – payments side

Date	Details	Bank (£)	VAT (£)	Trade payables (£)	Repairs (£)	Stationery (£)
15/12/X7	Locksmiths r us	30.00				
18/12/X7	RMT Ltd.					
22/12/X7	Paperchain Ltd.					
24/12/X7						
Totals						

Task 7 (8 marks)

You are working on the receipts side of the cash book. For this task you may ignore VAT.

The following cash sales were counted and put into the safe.

Date	Details	Total (£)
20/12/X7	Cash Sales	42.00

The following amounts were received from credit customers.

Date	Customer	Payment Type	Total (£)
15/12/X7	Mayor & Sons	Faster Payment	655.90
22/12/X7	C Whelan	Cheque	224.60

Complete the receipts side of the cash book shown below.

Enter details into the relevant columns, and enter figures to complete each column.

Total each column and check your answer by cross casting your figures.

Cash book extract – receipts side

Details	Bank (£)	Cash (£)	Trade Receivables (£)	Cash Sales (£)
Mayor & Sons	655.90		655.90	
Cash Sales				
C Whelan				
Totals				

Task 8 (9 marks)

You have the following information about cash in hand.

Date	Details	Amount (£)
30/11/X7	Amount counted at the end of the day	180.00
4/12/X7	Cash sales	120.00
5/12/X7	Cash sales	75.00
10/12/X7	Paid for lunch for a meeting	30.00
19/12/X7	Paid for refreshments for the office	15.00
21/12/X7	Cash sales	143.00
23/12/X7	Paid a taxi fare	21.50
24/12/X7	Cash sales	70.00

a) Complete the table to calculate the closing amount of cash in hand on the 21st December. You do not need to use minus signs or brackets in your answer.

Cash in hand	£
Opening amount on 1st December 20X7	180.00
Total receipts	
Total payments	
Closing amount on 24th December 20X7	